60-Minute Recipes

100 Complete Meals for the Gourmet

Enrica Jarratt and Ermenegildo Muzzulini

BONANZA BOOKS
NEW YORK

Photographs were taken at the Hotel Cavalieri
Hilton and the Ristorante George's, Rome.

The publishers would like to thank the Leone
Limentani Co. and the Casa Danese, Rome,
for the loan of equipment for the photographs.

The publishers would also like to express their
gratitude to Contessa Luciana Rocchetti Besi
and Signora Maresa Valeriani for their help
with location photography.

Drawings
Maria Pozzi

Photographs
Mauro Pucciarelli

Cover photograph
Mario Rossi

Translated by Sara Harris.
Copyright © 1975 by Arnoldo Mondadori Editore
S.p.A., Milan
English translation copyright © 1984 Arnoldo
Mondadori Editore S.p.A., Milan

This 1984 edition published by Bonanza Books,
distributed by Crown Publishers, Inc.

Printed in Spain by Artes Gráficas Toledo, S.A.

D. L. TO: 764-1984

Library of Congress Cataloging in Publication Data

Jarratt, Enrica
  60-minute recipes.
Translation of: 100 Menu in Sessanta Minuti

Includes index.

1. Cookery, international. 2. Menus. I. Muzzulini,
Ermenegildo. II. Title. III. Sixty-minute recipes.

TX725.A1J3413   1984   641.5'55   84-6476

ISBN 0-517-439344

h g f e d c b a

For each menu titles printed in bold are those for which recipes are provided. Suggested accompaniments appear in lighter print.

Measurements are given in US cups, imperial and metric. Since conversions are working approximations, never mix measurements: use either US, imperial or metric for each recipe. British spoons are slightly larger than American and metric, so where quantities are given in tablespoons the larger refers to American and metric and the smaller to British. When measuring very small quantities or with teaspoons the difference is negligible.

All recipes serve four.

Each complete menu is designed to take a total preparation time of sixty minutes, though preparation times may vary slightly depending on the speed at which each individual cook works.

Foreword

The ever-increasing wealth of books and magazines on cooking and entertaining has fostered the taste for fine food among a wider public so that today people are rediscovering the pleasure of eating in style at home. Cooking is an art which, like painting and music, both educates and broadens the mind, enhancing one's perceptions by appealing to the senses. Food must therefore be thoughtfully chosen and skilfully prepared so that it satisfies not only our sense of taste but also our sense of smell and sight.

Good cooking as we understand it today is the result of centuries of culinary experimentation: it makes the most of traditional, often ancient recipes which can now be prepared by new methods and in a shorter time than ever before.

This book will prove indispensable for all cooks and lovers of good food who enjoy keeping open house for unexpected guests, welcoming old friends or simply preparing something special for the family.

This collection of menus also provides an opportunity for the enthusiastic cook to improve his knowledge and culinary expertise by using both new and familiar ingredients. The different dishes are grouped together to form complete and well balanced menus in which both homemade and commercially prepared foodstuffs are used. Fresh ingredients are combined with top-quality canned, frozen and processed foods, reconciling the principles of a healthy diet with the constraints of a busy life.

This book was compiled by Enrica Jarratt of George's restaurant in Rome and by Ermenegildo Muzzulini, Chef d'Hôtel of the Rome Hilton. Both authors belong to the Commanderie des Cordons Bleus de France and are both masters in the art of international haute cuisine. Each menu reflects the vast experience and expertise of the authors whose enthusiasm and genuine love of gastronomy cannot fail to communicate itself to the reader.

L. Carnacina

60-Minute Recipes

Provisions to keep in store

Wines and spirits used in cooking

Although it is not strictly necessary to buy the most expensive spirits or the finest wines for cooking, it is important to choose reliable names and avoid inferior brands.

Brandy
Rum
Grand Marnier
Marsala (Madeira can be substituted, with satisfactory results)
Madeira (Marsala can be substituted, but with slightly less satisfactory results)
Maraschino
Dry sherry
Kirsch
Gin
Whisky
Armagnac (Cognac or brandy can be substituted)
Triple Sec
Anisette or Pernod (infrequently used in cooking)
Cointreau
Calvados (apple brandy; an excellent complement to veal and chicken dishes)
Dry white wine
Full-bodied red wine (such as Barolo or the more robust Chianti wines, etc.)

Fresh herbs to grow in your garden or indoors

Since it is often difficult to find fresh herbs in the shops or market, it is advisable to grow a few of the more commonly used plants at home. Use fresh herbs whenever possible: their taste and aroma is far superior to the dried variety.

Chervil

An annual similar to parsley but with a subtle aniseed flavour. Chervil is classified as one of the *fines herbes* and is a vital ingredient in Parmentier soup and many other dishes. Requires the same treatment as tarragon.

Chives

A perennial with a very mild taste of garlic but without the disadvantages caused by the essential oil contained in garlic. Delicious in salads and omelettes or mixed with sour cream, as in many Russian and Scandinavian dishes. In summer chives grow well in poor soil in a sunny spot with very little water; in winter they must be grown in cold frames or greenhouses or in a sunny kitchen window. They are propagated by dividing and replanting the clump of tiny onion roots at the base of the plant.

Mint

Garden mint or spearmint should not be confused with peppermint, which has rounded, more downy leaves. The wide, sharp-pointed leaves are used in refreshing long drinks and for garnishing both sweet and savoury dishes. Excellent cooked with peas or new potatoes, steamed or boiled. A perennial herb requiring the same treatment as tarragon.

Parsley

Curled parsley has a more pronounced flavour than the broader-leaved variety and stays crisp and fresh for longer when used as a garnish. Very good fried. An annual plant, it should be grown in the same conditions as chives.

Tarragon

A perennial and one of the *fines herbes*. Tarragon has a delicate aniseed flavour that blends well with chicken; it is often used in salads and for making tarragon vinegar. In summer it should be grown in partial shade and should be watered every two days; in winter it will grow well indoors on a sunny window sill or in a heated greenhouse.

Essential vegetables and herbs:

Garlic
Onions
Chilli peppers
Shallots or scallions/spring onions
Potatoes
Sage
Bay leaves
Thyme
Rosemary

Basic supplies for the refrigerator:

Fresh butter
Clarified butter (see note below)*
Milk
Eggs
Parmesan cheese for grating, well wrapped in greaseproof paper or plastic wrap.

* Clarified butter is used for cooking at high temperature. The clarifying process separates the fat from the casein, the substance in butter which burns extremely easily, thus making the butter turn brown and indigestible. Clarified butter keeps for a considerable time without turning sour or rancid. Place plenty of butter in a wide bowl and heat in a bain marie for about 10 minutes once the butter has melted; the water in the bain marie should barely simmer. Skim off any impurities as they rise to the surface; leave the butter to stand for about 10 minutes before straining carefully into another bowl, taking care that the white deposit remains in the bottom of the original bowl. Alternatively, leave to cool and solidify, then scrape away the hardened sediment.

For the vegetable compartment:
1 carrot
1 stick celery
small bunch parsley, with the stalks immersed in water acidulated with lemon juice
lemons

Fresh meat and fish should be tightly wrapped in plastic wrap or greaseproof paper and placed in the refrigerator immediately. Meat and fish should never be placed in the freezer compartment unless they are to be deep-frozen, in which case they must be properly prepared.

For the store cupboard:
French mustard (Dijon)
Mustard powder
Tomato ketchup
Tabasco sauce
Worcestershire sauce
Chilli sauce
Soy sauce
Melba sauce
Curry powder
Cayenne pepper
Sweet paprika
Hot paprika
Chilli peppers
Red wine vinegar
White wine vinegar
Tarragon vinegar
Olive oil
Sunflower oil

White peppercorns
Black peppercorns
Cinnamon sticks
Ground cinnamon
Nutmeg
Oregano
Dried mushrooms
Saffron
Breadcrumbs
All-purpose/plain flour
Rice and pasta
Cornstarch/cornflour
Cocktail cherries
Cloves
Gelatine
Pickled capers
Meat essence/extract
Stock cubes
Vanilla pods kept in superfine/caster or confectioners'/icing sugar: stored in a sealed jar, the vanilla will flavour and scent the sugar.
Sugar
Long wooden or stainless steel skewers
Table salt
Cooking salt
Instant coffee
Cocoa powder
Chocolate chips
Sugar drops or hundreds-and-thousands
Apricot jam
Mixed candied fruit for cakes and desserts
Seedless white raisins/sultanas
Pine nuts
Almonds

MENU 1

Avodacos à la Ritz
Champagne risotto
Steak Diane
Mixed salad
Raspberries in orange juice

Shopping list

2 avocados ● 2 oranges ● mixed salad ingredients ● parsley ●
1 qt/1 lb/450 g frozen raspberries ● 1 small carton light/single
cream ● 4 3½-oz/100-g fillet steaks ● ¼ bottle Champagne ●
3 oz/80 g cooked canned shrimp/prawns ● 1 bottle shrimp/
prawn cocktail sauce or ingredients for making it (see p. 26) ●
1 lemon.

From the store cupboard ● butter – rice – onion
– 1 egg – stock – dry white wine – Dijon mustard
– Worcestershire sauce – olive oil – vinegar – salt
– pepper – clarified butter (see p. 11).

Work schedule ● Prepare the avocado starter
and place in the refrigerator. Start the risotto
and while it is cooking, wash the salad and
prepare the sauce for the Steak Diane.

Avocados à la Ritz

2 avocados
½ lemon
⅓ cup/3 oz/80 g cooked shrimp/prawns
¼ cup/2 fl oz/60 ml shrimp/prawn cocktail sauce,
bottled or homemade (see p. 26)
4 lettuce leaves

Slice the avocados lengthwise in half without
peeling them; remove the stone and brush the
flesh lightly with the lemon to prevent discolouration. Drain the shrimp/prawns well, mix
with the sauce and place a quarter of the mixture
in the hollow of each avocado. Chill in the
refrigerator for at least half an hour before
serving. Serve each avocado on a lettuce leaf.

Preparation: 5 minutes.
Refrigeration: 1 hour.

Champagne risotto

½ tbsp finely chopped onion
scant ½ cup/3½ oz/100 g butter
generous 1½ cups/12 oz/350 g risotto rice
⅔ cup/5 fl oz/150 ml dry white wine
*4¼ cups/1¾ pints/1 liter stock (made with light
stock cube if necessary, but well diluted and not
too salty)*
pepper
1 egg yolk
¼ bottle dry Champagne (brut), not chilled

Fry the onion gently in 2 tbsp/generous 1 oz/30 g
butter; add the rice and stir for a couple of
minutes over a high heat; add the white wine

and cook until it has evaporated; add half the
boiling stock and continue cooking for 16-18
minutes, according to the quality of the rice; add
small ladlefuls of stock as required, allowing the
rice to absorb the liquid each time before adding
more. Remove the risotto from the heat when
almost cooked and quite dry. Add the remaining butter, cut into small pieces; season with
freshly ground pepper, mix in the egg yolk and
stir vigorously with a wooden spoon. To serve:
transfer the risotto to a deep, heated oval
serving dish; carefully remove the wire holding
the cork in position and place the unopened
Champagne bottle upright in the center of the
risotto. Place the dish on the table and remove
the cork so that the Champagne cascades down
the sides of the bottle into the rice. For a more
spectacular effect, tap the bottom of the bottle
quite hard with a fork before placing it in the
middle of the risotto. Remove the bottle and stir
the Champagne into the rice before serving. No
grated Parmesan is served with this risotto.

Preparation: 35 minutes.

Steak Diane
(can be prepared at the table)

3 tsp Dijon mustard
1 tbsp chopped parsley
1 tsp Worcestershire sauce
salt
pepper
4/3 tbsp light/single cream
¼ cup/2 oz/50 g clarified butter
4 ¼-lb/3½-oz/100-g fillet steaks, lightly beaten

Begin by preparing the sauce: place the mustard, parsley, Worcestershire sauce, salt, and freshly ground pepper in a bowl and beat well with a fork; gradually pour in the cream. Heat the clarified butter; when hot add the steaks. Fry briefly on both sides, pour the sauce over the steaks and cook for another 20 seconds, turning the steaks twice more. Serve.

Preparation: 10 minutes.

MENU 2

Peppers with anchovies and garlic
Spaghetti alla carbonara
Escalopes de veau Cordon Bleu
Buttered French beans
Pears in red wine

Shopping list

8 2½-oz/70-g veal cutlets/escalopes ● 3½ oz/100 g cooked ham, thinly sliced ● 3½ oz/100 g Gruyère cheese, thinly sliced ● small bunch parsley ● 2 lemons ● 1 small carton light/single cream ● 4 large stewing pears ● 1 packet frozen French beans ● 4 oz/125 g cured salt bacon/belly of pork, thickly diced ● 1 small jar peppers (preferably red and yellow) ● 1 can anchovies ● 14 oz/400 g spaghetti ● 4 eggs.

From the store cupboard ● butter – garlic – Parmesan cheese – oil – salt – red wine – pepper – port – cinnamon – sugar – flour – breadcrumbs – sunflower oil.

Work schedule ● Prepare the pears and set them to cook. Prepare the starter. Prepare the veal for frying. Cook the beans. Put the spaghetti in to boil. Cook the cutlets/escalopes. Toss the beans in butter.

Peppers with anchovies and garlic

1 small jar peppers (preferably red and yellow)
1 can anchovies
1 clove garlic, cut into wafer-thin slices

Cut the drained peppers into 1-in/2.5-cm strips and arrange on small plates; place an anchovy fillet in the center and 3 slivers of garlic on top of each fillet.

Preparation: 5 minutes.

Spaghetti alla carbonara

14 oz/400 g spaghetti
a little salt
4 oz/125 g cured salt bacon/belly of pork, thickly diced
1 tbsp oil
3 eggs
2-3 tbsp freshly grated Parmesan or Pecorino cheese
2-3 tbsp light/single cream

plenty of freshly ground pepper
2½ tbsp/generous 1 oz/30 g butter

While the spaghetti is boiling in plenty of lightly salted water, fry the salt bacon/belly of pork in the oil. Place the eggs, cheese, cream, salt and pepper in a bowl and beat well. Heat the butter in a large deep frying pan. When the spaghetti is *al dente* (tender but still firm), drain and transfer to the frying pan; add the salt bacon/belly of pork and mix well. Add the contents of the bowl and cook over a low heat until the sauce is creamy and coats the spaghetti.

Preparation: 15 minutes from the time the spaghetti is added to the boiling water.

Escalopes de veau Cordon Bleu

8 2½-oz/70-g veal cutlets/escalopes
3½ oz/100 g cooked ham, thinly sliced
3½ oz/100 g Gruyère cheese, thinly sliced
3/2 tbsp flour
1 egg, beaten lightly with a fork
3/2 tbsp breadcrumbs
5/3 tbsp oil
2½ tbsp/generous 1 oz/30 g butter
salt
1 lemon, cut into 4 wedges
parsley

Place the cutlets/escalopes between dampened sheets of greaseproof paper and pound until very thin. Lay 4 cutlets/escalopes on the table and place a slice of ham and cheese on each, leaving a narrow border uncovered; lightly flour the outside edge, cover with the second slice of veal and press the edges together. Coat lightly with flour, dip in beaten egg and coat with breadcrumbs. Fry briskly in oil and butter, drain, sprinkle with salt on both sides and transfer to a serving dish. Garnish with lemon wedges and parsley.

Preparation: 30 minutes.

Pears in red wine

4 large stewing pears
3/2 tbsp sugar
1-2 tbsp port
⅔ cup/5 fl oz/150 ml red wine
2 cups/16 fl oz/450 ml water
1 tsp lemon juice
small piece lemon rind
small stick cinnamon

Peel the pears without removing the stalk and place upright in a tall narrow cooking pot. Add the remaining ingredients, cover and simmer very gently over a low heat for about 20 minutes or until tender. Transfer the pears carefully to a serving dish; boil the cooking liquid until it has reduced and slightly thickened and pour over the pears.

Preparation: 10 minutes.
Total time: 30 minutes.

MENU 3

Mushroom salad
Soupe à l'oignon
Bombay hamburgers
Creamed spinach
Fruit salad

Shopping list

5 oz/150 g button mushrooms ● 2¼ lb/1 kg onions ● 1¼ lb/ 600 g lean ground/minced beef and scant ½ cup/3½ oz/ 100 g fresh grated suet or 4 ready-made hamburgers ● 2|lb/900 g frozen spinach ● scant 1 cup/5 fl oz/150 ml light/single cream ● 1 lemon ● 1 can fruit salad ● 1 small loaf of bread ● 4 oz/125 g Gruyère cheese ● 1 jar mango chutney.

From the store cupboard ● butter – stock – nutmeg – flour – chilli sauce – sugar – liqueur or fresh orange juice for the fruit salad – olive oil – salt – pepper – sherry – sunflower oil – curry powder.

Work schedule ● Slice and dress the mushrooms and chill in the refrigerator. Sprinkle the fruit salad with liqueur or fresh orange juice and place in the refrigerator. Turn on the oven. Fry the onions in an open pressure cooker. Turn off the oven and place the thick slices of bread inside to dry. Cook the spinach. Finish preparing the onion soup. Drain and season the spinach. Cook the hamburgers.

Mushroom salad

5 oz/150 g button mushrooms
lemon juice
olive oil
salt
pepper

Rinse and dry the mushrooms. Using the caps only, slice very thinly with a mandoline cutter or truffle slicer. Sprinkle immediately with lemon juice, olive oil, salt and pepper. Refrigerate for at least half an hour before serving.

Preparation: 15 minutes.
Refrigeration: 1 hour.

Soupe à l'oignon
(pressure cooker method)

2¼ lb/1 kg onions
2½ tbsp/generous 1 oz/30 g butter
½ tbsp flour
4/3 tbsp sherry
4¼ cups/1¾ pints/1 liter beef stock
1 small loaf of bread, cut into thick slices and dried in the oven
1 cup/4 oz/125 g Gruyère cheese, grated

15

Opposite:
Menu 1, page 13

Slice the onions into very thin rings and fry gently in the butter in an open pressure cooker until golden brown. Stir in the flour and cook for a few seconds; add the sherry and allow to evaporate; pour in the hot stock, close the pressure cooker, bring to pressure and cook for 10 minutes. Pour the soup into 4 ovenproof bowls and place slices of bread in each; sprinkle with the cheese and place under the broiler/grill for a few minutes.

Preparation: 30 minutes.

Bombay hamburgers

2¹/₂ cups/1¹/₄ lb/600 g lean ground/minced beef
scant ¹/₂ cup/3¹/₂ oz/100 g freshly grated suet
1-2 tbsp cold water
salt
pepper
(or 4 ready-made hamburgers)
¹/₂ tbsp sunflower oil
4/3 tbsp mango chutney
1 tsp curry powder
a few drops chilli sauce

Mix the ground/minced beef and suet together with the water and season with salt and pepper; shape into 4 hamburgers 1¹/₄ in/3 cm thick; brush lightly with oil and cook on the griddle or in a frying pan with no added oil until they are rare, medium or well done, according to preference. Transfer to a serving dish. Heat the mango chutney with the curry powder and chilli sauce and pour over the hamburgers.

Preparation: 15 minutes.

Creamed spinach

2 lb/900 g frozen spinach
2¹/₂ tbsp/generous 1 oz/30 g butter
salt
pepper
pinch sugar
nutmeg
scant 1 cup/5 fl oz/150 ml light/single cream

Cook the spinach according to the manufacturer's instructions; drain well and chop very coarsely. Melt the butter and add the spinach: season with salt, pepper, sugar and freshly grated nutmeg. Add the cream, bring to the boil and simmer gently for 5-6 minutes. If the spinach becomes a little dry, add a little extra butter.

Preparation: 20 minutes.

MENU 4

Prosciutto/raw ham with melon or figs
Seafood curry
Lamb chops with lemon and rosemary
Mixed green salad
Pineapple with kirsch

Shopping list

8 oz/250 g prosciutto/raw ham ● 3 oz/80 g canned shrimp/prawns ● 3 oz/80 g canned clams ● 3 oz/80 g canned mussels ● 1¹/₄ lb/600 g lamb chops, ³/₄ in/1.5 cm thick ● 1 melon or 12-16 fresh figs ● 1 pineapple ● parsley ● mixed salad ingredients ● 2 ripe tomatoes or 4 large mushrooms ● 15 blanched almonds ● 1 small carton light/single cream ● powdered rosemary.

From the store cupboard ● butter – curry powder – dry sherry or dry vermouth – rice – lemon – kirsch for the pineapple – sugar – oil – vinegar – salt – pepper – flour.

Work schedule ● Peel and slice the pineapple, discarding the hard central core. Sprinkle with kirsch and chill in the refrigerator. Prepare the melon or figs and place in the refrigerator. Trim and wash the salad. Prepare the Seafood curry, starting with the rice. Broil/grill the lamb chops.

Opposite:
Menu 4, page 16

Prosciutto/raw ham with melon or figs

8 oz/250 g prosciutto/raw ham, very thinly sliced
1 ripe melon or 12-16 fresh ripe figs
4 sprigs parsley

Arrange the prosciutto/raw ham on one side of a large serving platter and the melon slices (seeds and peel removed) on the other; if figs are used, carefully peel off the outer skin. Garnish with sprigs of parsley.

Preparation: 10 minutes.

Seafood curry

1½ cups/11 oz/325 g rice
3 tbsp/1½ oz/40 g butter
½-1 tbsp flour
1 tsp curry powder
½ cup/3½ fl oz/100 ml light/single cream
scant ½ cup/3½ fl oz/100 ml water or clam juice
15 blanched almonds, chopped
3 oz/80 g canned shrimp/prawns
3 oz/80 g canned clams
3 oz/80 g canned mussels
2-3 tbsp dry sherry or dry vermouth
salt
pepper

Boil the rice in salted water, drain well and arrange in a ring on a hot serving platter. While the rice is cooking, prepare the curry:
Melt the butter in a heavy saucepan, stir in the flour and cook briefly until light brown in colour; add the curry powder and cook a little longer. Remove from the heat, stir in the cream and water or clam juice and return to the heat. Stir continuously until the sauce boils. Add the almonds and cook for a further 2 minutes. Add the seafood and the sherry or vermouth and season with salt and pepper; once the sauce has returned to the boil, pour into the center of the rice ring.

Preparation: 20 minutes.

Lamb chops with lemon and rosemary

a few drops lemon juice
powdered rosemary
1¼ lb/600 g lamb chops, ¾ in/1.5 cm thick
oil
salt
pepper
4 broiled/grilled tomato halves or 4 mushroom caps
a few sprigs parsley

Rub a little lemon juice and powdered rosemary into the lamb chops. Preheat the broiler/grill and lightly oil the grill pan. Broil/grill the chops for 2-4 minutes on each side. Transfer to a heated serving dish, season with salt and pepper and garnish with the broiled/grilled tomato halves or mushrooms and a few sprigs of parsley.

Preparation: 10 minutes.

MENU 5

Smoked salmon
Cream of spinach soup
Hawaiian ham
Sautéed potatoes
Peaches flamed in rum

Shopping list

10½ oz/300 g smoked salmon ● 2 9-oz/250-g slices cooked ham, ¾ in/2 cm thick ● 1 small carton light/single cream ● 4 eggs ● 2¼ lb/1 kg fresh or 1¾ lb/800 g frozen spinach ● 1 loaf brown bread ● ½ loaf white bread ● 1 can pineapple rings ● 1 can peach halves ● 2 lemons ● 1 orange ● 2¼ lb/1 kg potatoes ● parsley ● 1 packet brown sugar.

From the store cupboard ● butter – cayenne pepper – flour – stock – freshly grated Parmesan cheese – oil – cocktail cherries – sugar – brandy – dark rum.

Work schedule ● Boil the potatoes. Prepare the Cream of spinach soup; do not thicken until the last minute. Place the bread in the oven to dry. Prepare the Hawaiian ham and sautéed potatoes. Set out the ingredients for the Peaches flamed in rum.

Smoked salmon

Smoked salmon is traditionally garnished with lemon wedges and cayenne pepper and served with slices of buttered brown bread.

Cream of spinach soup

2¼ lb/1 kg fresh or 1¾ lb/800 g frozen spinach
3 tbsp/1½ oz/40 g butter
salt
pepper
velouté sauce (made with ¼ cup + 3 tbsp/scant 1½ oz/35 g flour, 3 tbsp/scant 1½ oz/35 g butter, 1½ cups/12 fl oz/350 ml light stock)
4¼ cups/1¾ pints/1 liter light stock
4 egg yolks
⅔ cup/4 fl oz/125 ml light/single cream
3/2 tbsp freshly grated Parmesan cheese
thick slices of white bread

Cook the spinach and drain well; liquidize and heat gently in 1½ tbsp/scant 1 oz/20 g butter. Season with salt and pepper. Combine the velouté sauce and the stock, bring to the boil and simmer for a few minutes, stirring continuously. Add the spinach. Just before serving add the egg yolks, lightly beaten with the cream, and bring almost to the boil. Remove from the heat, sprinkle in half the grated Parmesan and pour into a heated soup tureen. Cut the bread into cubes and dry them in the oven; fry until golden brown in the remaining butter and sprinkle with the remaining Parmesan cheese.

Preparation: 15 minutes.
Total time: 40 minutes.

Hawaiian ham

2 9-oz/250-g slices cooked ham, ¾ in/2 cm thick, cut in half
2½ tbsp/generous 1 oz/30 g butter or a little oil
2 canned pineapple rings, cut in half
1½-2 tbsp brown sugar
4 cocktail cherries
a few sprigs parsley

Brush the ham lightly with oil and broil/grill or fry in butter, allowing 3 minutes for each side. Sprinkle the pineapple rings with brown sugar and place under the broiler/grill to caramelize and glaze the surface of the fruit. Heat the cherries very slightly. Arrange the ham slices on a heated serving platter and place a pineapple ring and a cherry in the center of each. Garnish with a few sprigs of parsley.

Preparation: 15 minutes.

Peaches flamed in rum
(can be prepared at the table)

small knob of butter
¼ cup/2 oz/50 g brown sugar
small piece orange peel
small piece lemon peel
3/2 tbsp orange juice
1 tbsp brandy
8 canned peach halves
3/2 tbsp dark rum

Place the butter, sugar, orange and lemon peel in a frying pan over a low heat, stirring with the orange peel speared on a fork. As soon as the sugar turns golden, gradually add the orange juice and the brandy; continue to stir until well blended. Add the drained peaches to the frying pan and turn several times until they are heated through. When the sugar has caramelized, add the rum, heat and then flame, shaking the pan gently. Serve immediately.

Preparation: 6 minutes.

MENU 6

Smoked herring starter
Roast chicken with rosemary
Pommes de terre noisette
Mixed salad
Ice cream gâteau

Shopping list

2 1¾-lb/800-g oven-ready chickens ● 4 smoked herrings ● ½ loaf brown bread ● 2¼ lb/1 kg potatoes ● 2 small onions ● mixed salad ingredients ● parsley ● a few sprigs rosemary ● 1 small carton sour cream ● 1 frozen ice cream gâteau.

From the store cupboard ● stock – butter – Tabasco sauce or lemon juice – sunflower oil – olive oil – vinegar – salt – pepper.

Work schedule ● Prepare the chickens and place in the oven. Scoop out the potato balls and place in the oven. Wash the salad. Prepare the Smoked herring starter.

Smoked herring starter

3 tbsp/1½ oz/40 g butter
½ loaf brown bread, sliced
4 smoked herrings
½ cup/3½ fl oz/100 ml sour cream mixed with a few drops Tabasco sauce or lemon juice
onion rings, very thinly sliced

Butter the slices of bread and place a smoked herring on top; cover with a spoonful of sour cream and garnish with the raw onion rings.

Preparation: 10 minutes.

Roast chicken with rosemary

2 1¾-lb/800-g oven-ready chickens
salt
pepper
½ small onion
a few sprigs rosemary
2 small bunches parsley
4/3 tbsp sunflower oil
6 tbsp/3 oz/80 g butter

Wash and dry the chickens. Season with salt and pepper and put ¼ onion, a sprig of rosemary and a small bunch of parsley inside each bird. Truss the chickens, place in a roasting pan and sprinkle with oil. Roast in a hot oven (400°F/200°C/mk 6) for 40-50 minutes, depending on their size. When the chickens are tender, cut in half with poultry scissors, transfer to a heated serving dish and sprinkle with noisette butter (heat the butter until it is golden brown). Garnish with a sprig of fresh rosemary.

Preparation: 10 minutes.
Total time: 1 hour.

Pommes de terre noisette

2¼ lb/1 kg potatoes
6 tbsp/3 oz/80 g butter, melted
salt

Peel the potatoes and use a melon baller to scoop out small balls; place in a pan of cold water until needed to prevent discolouration. Drain and dry thoroughly, place in a roasting pan and pour the melted butter over the potato balls. Roast in the oven with the chicken for about 25 minutes; sprinkle with salt half way through cooking time and shake the pan occasionally to prevent the potato balls from sticking or browning unevenly.

Preparation: 15 minutes.
Total time: 35 minutes.

MENU 7

Chawan Mushi (Japanese chicken, fish and egg soup)
Fondue bourguignonne
Peach Melba

1¼ lb/600 g fillet or sirloin of beef ● 4 oz/125 g boned raw chicken breast ● 4 oz/125 g sole fillet ● 8 large shrimp/giant prawns ● 1 small can peach halves ● 4 Japanese mushroom caps (use dried *shiitake*, available from oriental stores) ● 3 eggs ● 1 lemon ● At least 4 sauces from the selection given in the Fondue bourguignonne recipe ● 12 oz/350 g vanilla ice cream ● 1 small bottle *mirin* (sweet rice wine) or dry sherry and sugar (allow 1½ tbsp to each ¼ cup/2 fl oz/60 ml sherry) ● instant *dashi* powder or fish stock cubes ● generous 1 oz/30 g toasted flaked almonds ● 1 bottle Melba sauce ● parsley or a few French beans.

From the store cupboard ● monosodium glutamate (optional) – rice – vegetable or sunflower oil – salt – soy sauce (preferably *shoyu* – Japanese light soy sauce).

Work schedule ● Prepare the Chawan Mushi. Boil the rice. Prepare the meat for the Fondue bourguignonne and set up the fondue equipment in the center of the table, together with a selection of sauces in small bowls. Prepare the Peach Melba and place in the coldest part of the refrigerator.

Chawan Mushi (Japanese chicken, fish and egg soup)

3 eggs
3¼ cups/1¼ pints/800 ml dashi *(Japanese basic stock, available in powdered form) or fish or chicken stock*
1 tsp Japanese soy sauce
1 tsp mirin *(see shopping list)*
salt
pinch monosodium glutamate (optional)
4 oz/125 g boned raw chicken breast, cut into strips
4 oz/125 g sole fillet, cut into oblique slices
4 small pieces lemon rind
8 large shrimp/giant prawns
4 dried shiitake *(Japanese mushroom caps), presoaked for 30 minutes in boiling water*
boiled rice
garnish:
4 small strips lemon rind
1 sprig parsley or 4 French beans

Break the eggs into a bowl and beat in the hot *dashi* or fish or chicken stock, the soy sauce, *mirin*, salt and monosodium glutamate. Strain through a fine sieve and ladle equal quantities into 4 cups or bowls. Distribute the pieces of chicken and sole, lemon rind, shrimp/prawns and mushrooms equally. Partly cover each cup or bowl with foil or a lid and cook in a bain marie in the oven at 325°F/170°C/mk 3 for 25 minutes.

Garnish with lemon rind and parsley or French beans and cook for another 5 minutes. Serve very hot boiled rice separately.

Preparation: 15 minutes.
Total time: 45 minutes.

Fondue bourguignonne

1¼ lb/600 g fillet or sirloin of beef
2¼ cups/18 fl oz/500 ml vegetable or sunflower oil
At least 4 of the following sauces, arranged in small bowls around the fondue stove: mayonnaise, vinaigrette, sauce diable, piccalilli, tomato ketchup, hot chilli-flavoured ketchup, curry sauce, barbecue sauce, tartare sauce, etc.

Trim off any fat, membrane or gristle from the meat and cut into ¾-in/2-cm cubes. Divide into 4 equal portions and place a small dish of meat in front of each guest. Place the fondue pot on the stove in the center of the table and make sure the flame is high enough to keep the oil boiling throughout the meal.

Preparation: 30 minutes.

Peach Melba

4 canned peach halves, drained
8 scoops vanilla ice cream
4 tbsp Melba sauce
1/4 cup/generous 1 oz/30 g toasted flaked almonds

Place a portion of ice cream in 4 crystal bowls or champagne glasses. Top each with a peach half, pour over the Melba sauce and sprinkle with the toasted flaked almonds.

Preparation: 5 minutes.

MENU 8

Smoked trout with horseradish sauce
Beef Stroganoff
Creamed potatoes
Ice cream and strawberries

Shopping list

4 smoked trout ● 1¼ lb/600 g fillet of beef ● 1 large horseradish root or 1 jar horseradish sauce ● 2 cucumbers or 1 small cos lettuce ● 1 small carton sour cream ● 1 small carton heavy/double cream ● 2¼ lb/1 kg potatoes ● 1 tube tomato paste ● 10 oz/275 g fresh or frozen strawberries ● 12 oz/350 g vanilla ice cream ● 2 eggs.

From the store cupboard ● butter – milk – flour – small piece onion – 1 shallot – dry sherry – stock – mustard powder – salt – pepper – fresh breadcrumbs – sugar – vinegar.

Work schedule ● Make the horseradish sauce. Boil the potatoes. Skin the smoked trout and place in the refrigerator. Set out the ingredients for the Beef Stroganoff. Wash and hull the strawberries and chill in the refrigerator.

Smoked trout with horseradish sauce

4 smoked trout
2 cucumbers or 1 small cos lettuce
horseradish sauce, freshly made (see recipe right)
or commercially prepared

Remove the head and backbone of the skinned trout; open the fish flat and serve on individual plates on a bed of thinly sliced cucumber rounds or strips of lettuce. Serve the horseradish sauce separately.

Preparation: 10 minutes.

Horseradish sauce
(excellent with roast beef and smoked fish)

6/4 tbsp finely grated horseradish root
6/4 tbsp lightly whipped cream
2-3 tbsp fresh breadcrumbs
2 hard-boiled egg yolks, mashed with a fork
pinch salt
1 tsp sugar
1 tbsp vinegar

Blend the ingredients together thoroughly to make a smooth and fairly thick sauce.

Preparation: 10 minutes.

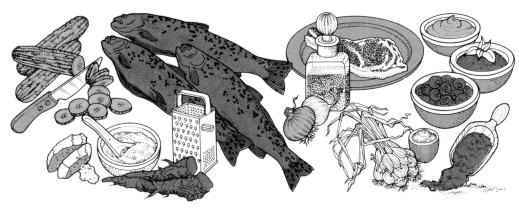

Beef Stroganoff

1½-2 tbsp flour
1¼ lb/600 g fillet of beef, cut into short narrow strips
6 tbsp/3 oz/80 g butter
small piece onion, finely chopped
1 shallot, finely chopped
1½-2 tbsp dry sherry
1½-2 tbsp tomato paste or homemade tomato sauce
1 level tsp mustard powder mixed with a little cold stock or water
⅔ cup/5 fl oz/150 ml stock
salt
pepper
6/4 tbsp sour cream

Flour the strips of meat very lightly and seal rapidly in very hot butter. The meat should just change colour. Remove the meat with a slotted spoon, drain well and set aside between two heated plates to keep warm. Add the chopped onion and shallot to the butter in the frying pan and brown; add the sherry and cook until it has partly evaporated before adding the tomato paste or sauce; cook over a light heat for 30 seconds. Stir in the mustard, stock, salt and pepper. Simmer for 2 minutes, then add the sour cream; bring almost to boiling point, add the beef strips and cook for a further 5 seconds. Cover the frying pan, draw aside from the heat and leave to stand for 3 minutes before serving.

Preparation: 15 minutes.

MENU 9

Crabe à la russe
Chilli con carne
Bananas flamed in kirsch

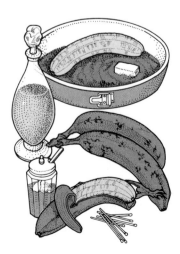

Shopping list

1 7-oz/200-g can crabmeat • 1 can diced mixed vegetables • 1 lb/450 g canned red kidney beans • 1 jar mayonnaise • 1 lettuce • small bunch parsley • 14 oz/400 g finely ground/minced lean beef • 1 14-oz/400-g can tomatoes • 6 bananas • kirsch • 1 lemon.

From the store cupboard • olive oil – 1 onion – oregano – chilli peppers – hot paprika – sugar – butter – salt – pepper – Tabasco or chilli sauce.

Work schedule • Prepare the Crabe à la russe and chill in the refrigerator. Make the Chilli con carne. Just before serving the Chilli con carne, place the bananas in the oven.

Crabe à la russe

1 cup/7 oz/200 g crabmeat
1 can diced mixed vegetables
juice of ½ lemon
salt
freshly ground pepper
5/3 tbsp mayonnaise
chopped parsley
4 large lettuce leaves

Drain and flake the crabmeat with a fork and mix with the diced vegetables; dress with lemon juice, salt and pepper and mayonnaise. Mix well and chill in the refrigerator for 40 minutes. Sprinkle with chopped parsley and serve on a lettuce leaf on individual plates.

Preparation: 10 minutes.
Refrigeration: 40 minutes.

Chilli con carne

1 onion, finely chopped
5/3 tbsp olive oil
½ tsp paprika
pinch dried oregano
1 dried chilli pepper, finely chopped
1¾ cups/14 oz/400 g finely ground/minced lean beef
1 14-oz/400-g can tomatoes
½ tsp Tabasco or chilli sauce
1 lb/450 g canned red kidney beans
salt

Sauté the chopped onion in the oil: add the paprika, oregano and chilli pepper and cook for a few seconds. Add the ground/minced beef and sauté, breaking up any lumps with a wooden spoon, until the meat has browned. Add the tomatoes and the Tabasco or chilli sauce and cook for 3 minutes over a moderate heat. Stir in the drained red kidney beans, lower the heat, cover and cook for 45 minutes. Stir occasionally and add salt to taste. Serve in individual earthenware bowls.

Preparation: 50 minutes.

Bananas flamed in kirsch

6 bananas
3 tbsp/1½ oz/40 g butter
¼ cup/2 oz/50 g sugar
4/3 tbsp kirsch

Peel the bananas and cut in half lengthwise. Melt the butter in a shallow ovenproof dish, place the bananas in a single layer in the dish and sprinkle with sugar. Place in a hot oven (400°F/200°C/mk 6) for 5 minutes. Transfer the bananas to a heated serving dish: heat the kirsch in a small saucepan, set alight and pour quickly over the bananas. Shake the dish gently so that the kirsch flames freely.

Preparation: 10 minutes.

MENU 10

Melon with port
Sole fillets Florentine
Steamed spinach and potatoes
Hazelnut ice cream torte

Shopping list

4 fresh sole fillets (ask the fishmonger for the trimmings, skin and bones) ● 2¼ lb/1 kg fresh or 1¾ lb/800 g frozen spinach ● 2½ lb/1 kg new potatoes ● 1 small carton heavy/double cream ● 4 small melons ● 1 bottle port ● small bunch mint ● 1 hazelnut ice cream torte.

From the store cupboard ● butter – cocktail cherries – Parmesan cheese – flour – milk – dried mushrooms (Italian *porcini* or French *cèpes*) – white wine – salt – peppercorns.

Work schedule ● Start preparing the fumet. Prepare the melon and place in the refrigerator to chill. Make the Mornay sauce. Steam the spinach and the potatoes. Prepare the Sole fillets Florentine. Toss the spinach in butter.

Melon with port

4 small melons
1 cup/8 fl oz/225 ml port
4 cocktail cherries
8 leaves fresh mint

Place the melons with their stalks uppermost and slice off a small section of the top. Carefully scoop out the seeds; make a series of deep, fan-shaped incisions with a metal spoon into the flesh of the melon, spacing the incisions about 1½ in/4 cm apart. Place each melon in a small bowl; use half the port and pour a little into each melon. Chill in the refrigerator for at least 45 minutes. Before serving, pour off the port and any excess juice, and pour in the remaining fresh port. Garnish with the cocktail cherries and mint leaves. For a more decorative effect save the piece sliced off the top and affix it to the lower half with a cocktail stick so that it looks like an umbrella.

Preparation: 15 minutes.
Refrigeration: 45 minutes.

Sole fillets Florentine

1 cup/9 fl oz/250 ml Mornay sauce (basic white sauce with added heavy/double cream and freshly grated Parmesan cheese to make the sauce thicker)
12 new potatoes
butter
4 fresh sole fillets (reserve the trimmings, skin and bones for the fumet)
salt
3/2 tbsp white wine
½ cup/4 fl oz/125 ml water
1 dried mushroom (Italian porcini or French cèpes), presoaked
2¾ lb/1 kg fresh spinach, trimmed and washed or

1¾ lb/800 g frozen spinach
2-3 tbsp freshly grated Parmesan cheese

Make a fumet by simmering the reserved fish heads, trimmings and bones for 30 minutes.

Make the Mornay sauce. Steam the potatoes (see p. 40). Grease an ovenproof dish generously with butter; slightly flatten the fish with a meat bat or rolling pin and lay the fillets flat in the bottom of the dish; sprinkle with a little salt. Mix 6/4 tbsp of the fumet with the white wine and water; pour the liquid over the fish and add the mushroom. Cover the dish with greaseproof paper and place in a preheated oven (350°F/ 180°C/mk 4) for 10-15 minutes or until the fish fillets are cooked. Meanwhile steam the spinach until tender, drain thoroughly and chop coarsely; heat the spinach in a saucepan with a little butter over a gentle heat for about 5 minutes. Transfer to a heated serving platter. drain the fillets and place on the bed of spinach; spoon the Mornay sauce over the fish, covering each fillet but not the surrounding spinach. Arrange the steamed potatoes between the fish fillets. Sprinkle with freshly grated Parmesan cheese and a little melted butter. Place briefly under a preheated broiler/grill to brown lightly.

Preparation: 30 minutes.
Total time: 1 hour.

MENU   11

Scampi cocktail
Breaded chicken breasts
Buttered spinach
Assorted cheeses
Irish coffee

Shopping list

8 oz/225 g scampi tails or 2¼ lb/1 kg raw scampi • 4 medium-sized boned chicken breasts • 1 jar mayonnaise • 1 small lettuce • 2¼ lb/1 kg spinach • 1 lemon • small bunch parsley • 1 tomato • 1 small loaf white bread • 1 small carton heavy/double cream • assorted cheeses.

From the store cupboard • butter – tomato ketchup – tomato paste or homemade Italian tomato sauce – Worcestershire sauce – brandy – Tabasco sauce – cayenne pepper – flour – strong instant or strong black coffee – sugar – Irish whiskey – salt – pepper.

Work schedule • Prepare the Scampi cocktail and chill in the refrigerator. Cook the spinach. Cook the Breaded chicken breasts. Sauté the drained spinach in butter.

Scampi cocktail

8 oz/225 g scampi tails or 2¼ lb/1 kg raw scampi
6 lettuce leaves
6/4 tbsp shrimp/prawn cocktail sauce (see recipe right)
parsley or hard-boiled egg

If raw scampi are used, boil for 5-6 minutes, allow to cool and then peel. Arrange the lettuce leaves in individual dishes; mix half the shrimp/

prawn cocktail sauce with the scampi and place a portion in each dish. Top with the remaining sauce and garnish with sprigs of parsley or a slice of hard-boiled egg.

Preparation (excluding time allowed for cooking scampi): 15 minutes.

Shrimp/prawn cocktail sauce

(for scampi cocktail and similar fish or chicken starters)

6/4 tbsp mayonnaise
1-2 tbsp tomato ketchup
1 tsp tomato paste
1 tsp Worcestershire sauce
1 tbsp brandy
4 drops Tabasco sauce
pinch cayenne pepper

Place all the ingredients in a small bowl and mix well together.

Breaded chicken breasts

4 medium-sized chicken breasts, boned
salt
pepper
1-2 tbsp flour

generous ¼ cup/2½ oz/60 g melted butter
fresh breadcrumbs, made from 8 slices of white bread
small bunch parsley
4 lemon wedges
1 tomato, quartered (optional)

Lightly pound the chicken breasts and season with salt and pepper. Dip in flour, then melted butter and finally breadcrumbs. Broil/grill or fry the chicken breasts, sprinkling occasionally with a little of the remaining melted butter until they turn golden brown. Alternatively, they can be cooked, in an uncovered dish, in a very hot oven (450°F/230°C/mk 8). Transfer to a heated serving platter and garnish with sprigs of parsley, lemon wedges and quarters of tomato.

Preparation: 20 minutes.

Irish coffee

¾ cup/5 fl oz/150 ml heavy/double cream
4 cups strong black coffee
4 tsp sugar
4 measures Irish whiskey

Beat the cream until it is fairly thick but can still be poured slowly. Pour the piping hot coffee into special Irish coffee glasses; add the sugar and whiskey and stir. Pour the cream over the back of a spoon, held just touching the surface of the coffee, so that the cream floats on the surface.

Preparation: 5 minutes.

MENU 12

Hot Vichyssoise
Prague croquettes
French-fried potatoes
Salad with Indian dressing
Ice cream fruit gâteau

Shopping list

9 oz/250 g cooked shoulder of ham ● 7 oz/200 g Fontina or Gruyère cheese ● 6 eggs ● 1 bottle barbecue sauce or tomato sauce ● 7 fl oz/200 ml heavy/double cream ● 1 lb/450 g leeks ● 2 medium-sized potatoes ● 1 packet frozen French-fried potatoes or 2¼ lb/1 kg potatoes ● mixed salad ingredients ● 1 frozen ice cream fruit gâteau.

From the store cupboard ● stock – butter – flour – breadcrumbs – oil for frying – olive oil – vinegar – salt – pepper – curry powder – mild paprika.

Work schedule ● Start the preparation of the Vichyssoise. Wash and dry the salad. Make the Prague croquettes and place ready for frying. Fry the potatoes and then the croquettes.

Hot Vichyssoise

1 lb/450 g leeks
2 medium-sized potatoes
¼ cup/2 oz/50 g butter
4½ cups/1¾ pints/1 liter chicken stock
2 egg yolks
1¼ cups/7 fl oz/200 ml heavy/double cream
salt

Clean the leeks thoroughly and discard the green end leaves. Chop the leeks and the potatoes finely and sauté very gently in the butter until the leeks are soft. Pour in the boiling stock and simmer over a very low heat, tightly

covered, for 35 minutes. Liquidize the mixture in a food blender and then push through a fine sieve. Return the soup to the saucepan, stir in the egg yolks, mixed with the cream, and reheat gently almost to boiling point. Add salt to taste.

Preparation: 10 minutes.
Total time: 1 hour.

27

Prague croquettes

9 oz/250 g cooked shoulder of ham, cut into 6 thick slices
7 oz/200 g Fontina or Gruyère cheese
1 tsp mild paprika
2-3 tbsp flour
2 eggs
breadcrumbs
barbecue sauce or tomato sauce
oil for frying

Cut each slice of ham in half and cut the cheese into 12 fairly thick strips. Sprinkle the cheese with paprika and wrap a slice of ham around each strip, securing with a wooden cocktail stick if necessary; make sure that the cheese is properly enveloped by the ham. Dip the ham and cheese rolls in flour, then in beaten egg and then coat with breadcrumbs; deep fry for 7-8 minutes or until golden brown. Serve the sauce separately in a sauceboat.

Preparation: 15 minutes.

Indian dressing for mixed salad

Place the following ingredients in a small bowl: 2 chopped hard-boiled eggs, 1 tsp curry powder, blended with oil and vinegar. Mix well; add salt and pepper to taste.

MENU 13

Corn on the cob
Bombay curried scampi
Pilaf rice
Peaches with ice cream and whisky

Shopping list

1-1¼ lb/500-600 g scampi tails or frozen peeled shrimp/prawns • 1 can peaches • 4 corn cobs, fresh or canned • 1 small carton light/single cream • 7 oz/200 g long grain rice • 2 onions • 1 small carton natural yogurt • fresh or ground ginger • 2 ripe tomatoes or 1 small can tomato paste • ingredients for the "sambals": 2 or 3 types of chutney – 1 banana – seedless white raisins/sultanas – almonds – poppadoms or deep-fried prawn crackers • 2 portions vanilla ice cream.
Note: "sambal" is the generic term for the wide variety of accompaniments served with oriental dishes. Sambals may provide a bland contrast to the highly spiced main dish or they may be very spicy. They are usually arranged in small dishes or in one large dish with several sections. Each guest serves himself from the selection offered.

From the store cupboard • butter – garlic – chilli peppers – salt – pepper – stock – ground ginger – whisky – curry powder – oil.

Work schedule • Place the peaches in the refrigerator to chill. Fry the onion for the curry but do not proceed further at this stage. Prepare the sambals. Start cooking the Pilaf rice. If fresh corn is used, boil the cobs. Finish the Bombay curried scampi.

Corn on the cob

4 corn cobs, fresh or canned
scant ½ cup/3½ oz/100 g melted butter
salt
pepper

Remove the stalk and strip the leaves from each cob; discard any silky threads. Plunge the cobs into fast-boiling, unsalted water and boil for 20-30 minutes until the corn kernels are tender. Drain and transfer to a heated serving dish; insert a corn cob holder or small skewer into each end of the cobs. Season the melted butter with salt and pepper and serve separately in a sauceboat or jug.

Preparation: 10 minutes.
Total time: 40 minutes.

Bombay curried scampi

1 onion, thinly sliced
oil
1 clove garlic
½ chilli pepper
2 ripe tomatoes or 1 tbsp tomato paste
small piece fresh ginger root or ½ tsp ground ginger
¼ cup/2 oz/50 g butter
1 small carton natural yogurt
1-1¼ lb/500-600 g scampi tails or frozen peeled shrimp/prawns
1½-2 tbsp curry powder
salt
⅔ cup/4 fl oz/125 ml light/single cream
Serve with a selection of sambals:
sliced banana
seedless white raisins/sultanas
toasted flaked almonds
2 or 3 types of chutney
fried poppadoms
deep-fried prawn crackers

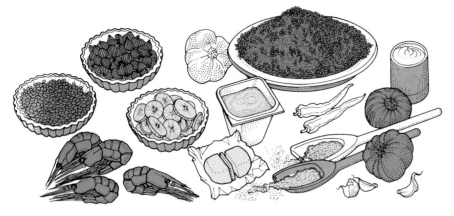

Pilaf rice
(basic recipe)

1 tbsp finely chopped onion
3 tbsp/1½ oz/40 g butter
1 cup/7 oz/200 g long grain rice
1¾ cups/¾ pint/400 ml hot stock

Fry the onion gently in an ovenproof casserole in half the butter without letting it brown. When it is translucent, add the rice and stir well for a minute or two. Add the hot stock, bring to the boil and cover the casserole tightly. Cook in a preheated oven (350°F/180°C/mk 4) without stirring for 20-30 minutes or until the rice is tender. Transfer to a heated serving dish, stir in the remaining butter, using two forks to separate the grains.

Preparation: 10 minutes.
Total time: 30 minutes.

Deep fry the sliced onion in hot oil until crisp and golden. Remove from the oil and drain well. Grind/mince or chop the fried onion, garlic, chilli pepper, tomatoes and ginger. Melt the butter, add the ground/minced ingredients and the yogurt; simmer for 4 minutes, then add the scampi or shrimp/prawns, the curry powder and salt to taste. Cook for a further 5 minutes, pour in the cream, lower the heat and simmer for 10 minutes. Transfer to a deep serving dish and serve the pilaf rice and sambals separately.

Preparation: 15 minutes.
Total time: 40 minutes.

MENU 14

Spaghetti with garlic, oil and chilli pepper
Steak au poivre
Mimosa salad
Crêpes Suchard

Shopping list

14 oz/400 g spaghetti ● 4 8-oz/225-g fillet or entrecôte steaks ● white peppercorns ● black peppercorns ● 3 eggs ● small bunch parsley ● mixed salad ingredients ● 3½ oz/100 g cooking chocolate ● 1 oz/25 g chocolate hundreds-and-thousands ● 9 fl oz/250 ml heavy/double cream ● 9 fl oz/250 ml milk.

From the store cupboard ● garlic – oil – clarified butter (see p. 11) – flour – salt – sugar – vinegar – pepper – chilli pepper.

Work schedule ● Make the crêpes and keep them warm between two plates over a saucepan of hot, not boiling, water. Boil 2 eggs and crush the peppercorns. Wash and drain the salad, transfer to a salad bowl and sprinkle with the sieved hard-boiled egg yolks. Grate or chop the chocolate. While the spaghetti is cooking, whip the cream and set out the ingredients for the Steak au poivre.

Spaghetti with garlic, oil and chilli pepper

14 oz/400 g spaghetti
salt
2 cloves garlic, thinly sliced
small piece dried chilli pepper, crumbled
4/3 tbsp oil
1 tbsp chopped parsley

While the spaghetti is boiling in plenty of salted water, sauté the garlic and chilli pepper in the oil in a small saucepan with a pinch of salt. Drain the spaghetti, return to the pan and pour over the chilli dressing. Sprinkle with chopped parsley.

Preparation: 15 minutes from the time the spaghetti is added to the boiling water.

Steak au poivre
(can be cooked at the table)

4 8-oz/225-g fillet or entrecôte steaks
1 clove garlic
salt
1-2 tbsp mixed black and white peppercorns, coarsely crushed
3 tbsp/1½ oz/40 g clarified butter

Do not pound the steaks or remove any surrounding fat. Pierce the meat at intervals. Gently scrape the surface of the meat with a fork and rub lightly with garlic; sprinkle with plenty of salt and crushed peppercorns, pressing well into the meat with the back of a wooden spoon. Brown the steaks over a high heat in the hot clarified butter. When the meat is sealed on both sides, lower the heat and cook gently for 5-12 minutes, according to preference, turning once only. Cover the pan, remove from the heat and leave for 7 minutes before serving.

Preparation: 15 minutes.

Mimosa salad

mixed green salad
2 hard-boiled egg yolks, sieved
3/2 tbsp oil
1 tbsp vinegar
salt
pepper

Dress the salad with the oil and vinegar and garnish with the egg yolks, which should be sieved directly over the salad.

Quick pancakes

scant 1 cup/3½ oz/100 g flour
generous 1 cup/9 fl oz/250 ml cold milk
1 egg
pinch salt
pinch superfine/caster sugar
1 tbsp sunflower oil
a little melted butter for frying the pancakes

Combine all the ingredients in the blender for 2 minutes; the batter can be used immediately. Heat a heavy-bottomed frying pan; cover the pan with a thin layer of melted butter and pour in one-tenth of the batter. Tilt the frying pan so that the batter evenly covers the bottom. Turn the pancake when the underside is golden brown and lightly cook the other side. This quantity is sufficient for 10 medium-sized pancakes.
There is no need to store pancakes in the refrigerator; they will keep perfectly well for up to 2 days, placed between two plates and stored in a cool place.

Preparation: 20 minutes.

Crêpes Suchard

1½ cups/9 fl oz/250 ml heavy/double cream
¼ cup/1 oz/25 g confectioners'/icing sugar
3½ squares/3½ oz/100 g grated cooking chocolate
8 hot pancakes (see recipe above)

¹/₄ cup / 1 oz / 25 g chocolate hundreds-and-thousands
1 tbsp superfine/caster sugar

Whip the cream and sweeten with the confectioners'/icing sugar. Melt the chocolate in a double boiler over hot, not boiling, water; pour a little into the middle of each pancake,

then fold in half and then into quarters. Arrange on a heated serving platter; decorate with plenty of whipped cream and sprinkle with chocolate hundreds-and-thousands and superfine/caster sugar.

Preparation (with ready-made pancakes): 10 minutes, otherwise 30 minutes.

MENU 15

Thick oxtail soup
Hamburgers with pizzaiola sauce
Creamed potatoes
Mixed salad
Assorted cheeses

Shopping list

1 large can thick oxtail soup (4 servings) ● 1¼ lb/600 g ground/minced lean beef and 3½ oz/100 g shredded suet (or 4 ready-made hamburgers) ● pitted black olives ● 1 anchovy fillet ● 6 large tomatoes or 1 small can tomatoes ● small bunch parsley ● mixed salad ingredients ● assorted cheeses ● 1 can or packet instant creamed potatoes.

From the store cupboard ● sunflower oil – olive oil – chilli pepper – oregano – salt – pepper – vinegar – garlic – milk – butter – onion.

Work schedule ● Prepare the Pizzaiola sauce. Wash and drain the salad. Shape the 4 hamburgers; prepare the creamed potatoes. Heat the soup. Cook the hamburgers.

Hamburgers with pizzaiola sauce

2½ cups/1¼ lb / 600 g ground/minced lean beef and scant ¾ cup/3½ oz/100 g shredded suet (or 4 ready-made hamburgers)
1 tbsp cold water
salt
pepper
½ tbsp oil
6/4 tbsp thick pizzaiola sauce (see recipe below)
pitted black olives

Mix together the ground/minced beef, the suet, 1 tbsp cold water, salt and pepper; shape into 4 hamburgers 1 in/2.5 cm thick; brush lightly with oil and cook on the griddle or in a heavy frying pan until rare, medium or well done, according to preference. Top each hamburger with a little pizzaiola sauce and garnish with black olives.

Preparation: 15 minutes.

Pizzaiola sauce

1-2 tbsp finely chopped onion
3/2 tbsp oil
1 anchovy fillet, chopped
½ clove garlic, coarsely chopped
½ chilli pepper, coarsely chopped
6 large tomatoes or 1 small can tomatoes
salt
pepper
1 level tsp oregano
1-2 tsp chopped parsley

Fry the chopped onion in the oil until it turns a pale golden brown; add the chopped anchovy, garlic and chilli pepper. Fry for a few minutes then add the tomatoes and season with salt and pepper. Cover and simmer for 20 minutes. Just before serving, stir in the oregano and chopped parsley.

Preparation: 10 minutes.
Total time: 30 minutes.

MENU 16

Macaroni with four cheeses
Tournedos flamed in brandy
Brussels sprouts or French
beans tossed in butter
Copacabana banana fritters

Shopping list

4 6-oz/175-g tournedos steaks • 9 oz/250 g butter • 14 oz/400 g macaroni • 1 pint/500 ml milk • 2 oz/50 g each of the following cheeses: Edam or Gouda – Gruyère – Fontina or Emmental – mild Provolone • 4 oz/125 g Parmesan cheese • 4 large bananas • fresh sage leaves • 1½ lb/700 g Brussels sprouts or French beans.

From the store cupboard • flour – pepper – garlic – cognac – rum – 1 egg – oil for frying – vanilla flavoured confectioners'/icing sugar – salt – clarified butter (see p. 11).

Work schedule • Mix the batter for the banana fritters. Slice the bananas and soak in rum. Trim, wash and steam the Brussels sprouts or French beans. Cut the cheese into thin slices. Make the Macaroni with four cheeses. Toss the sprouts or beans in melted butter. Set the oil to heat in the deep fryer. Cook the tournedos steaks at the table. Fry the banana fritters just before serving.

Macaroni with four cheeses

14 oz/400 g macaroni
scant ½ cup/3½ oz/100 g butter
1 level tbsp flour
⅔ cup/5 fl oz/150 ml milk
½ cup/2 oz/50 g Edam or Gouda
½ cup/2oz/50 g Gruyère
½ cup/2oz/50 g Fontina or Emmental
½ cup/2oz/50 g mild Provolone
5/3 tbsp freshly grated Parmesan cheese
freshly ground pepper

Put the pasta to cook in plenty of boiling salted water. Cut the cheese into thin slices. Heat half the butter in a small heavy-bottomed saucepan, add half the flour and stir for 30 seconds. Draw aside from the heat; stir in the milk gradually, return to the heat and bring to the boil; lower the heat and simmer for 6-7 minutes. Remove from the heat, stir in the cheese, cover and leave to stand. When the pasta is *al dente* (tender but still firm) drain and add the remaining butter and plenty of freshly ground pepper. Return the cheese sauce to the heat for a few seconds; pour over the pasta, stir quickly and serve at once with freshly grated Parmesan cheese.

Preparation: 15 minutes.
Total time: 25 minutes.

Tournedos flamed in brandy
(can be cooked at the table)

3/2 tbsp clarified butter
4 6-oz/175-g tournedos steaks
4 fresh sage leaves
3/2 tbsp cognac
3 tbsp/1½ oz/40 g butter
salt
pepper
1 clove garlic

Heat the clarified butter in a frying pan; place the steaks in the pan and brown the first side. Turn the steaks, add the fresh sage leaves and brown the other side. When the steaks are cooked to the desired degree, drain off the

cooking juices; add the cognac, heat gently and flame. Remove from the heat, place a knob of butter on top of each steak, cover and leave for 5 minutes before serving.

Preparation: 8 minutes.

Copacabana banana fritters

4 large bananas
3-4 tbsp rum
coating batter for frying (see recipe opposite)
oil for frying
confectioners'/icing sugar

Cut the bananas into thick, oblique slices. Soak in rum for 15 minutes. Drain, dip in the batter and deep fry until crisp and golden brown. Drain well, arrange on a serving dish and sprinkle with confectioners'/icing sugar.

Preparation: 30 minutes.

Coating batter

1 cup/4 oz/125 g flour
pinch salt
1 egg
2/3 cup/5 fl oz/150 ml milk

Sift the flour and salt into a bowl. Beat in the egg with a wooden spoon and gradually stir in the milk. Beat well until the batter is smooth and the ingredients are well blended. Alternatively place all the ingredients in the liquidizer and blend for a few seconds.

MENU 17

Smoked mussels with brown bread and butter
Cream of pea soup
Chicken à la chasseur
Raspberry cheesecake

Shopping list

¾ lb/350 g frozen peas, 1¾ pints/1 liter milk and 9 fl oz/250 ml light/single cream, or 1 large can cream of pea soup ● 2 cans smoked mussels ● 1 loaf wholemeal bread ● 1 2¾-lb/1.2-kg chicken ● small bunch parsley ● chervil ● rosemary ● 7 oz/200 g button mushrooms ● 1 anchovy fillet ● ½ oz/10 g dried mushrooms ● 1 frozen raspberry cheesecake.

From the store cupboard ● flour – salt – pepper – sugar – garlic – oil – white wine – vinegar – butter – chilli pepper.

Work schedule ● Cut the chicken into 8 portions and brown gently. Prepare the white sauce. Proceed to the second stage of cooking the chicken. Make the Cream of pea soup. Clean and slice the mushrooms and sauté in butter.

Cream of pea soup

3 tbsp/1½ oz/40 g butter
¾ lb/350 g frozen peas
small bunch parsley with stalks
small bunch chervil with stalks
3 cups/1¼ pints/750 ml milk
pinch sugar
1½ cups/12 fl oz/350 ml white sauce
salt
pepper
1½ cups/9 fl oz/250 ml light/single cream
1 tbsp chopped parsley or chervil

Melt the butter in a heavy-bottomed saucepan; add the peas, the bunches of parsley and chervil, a few tbsp of milk and the sugar. Cook over a gentle heat until the peas are tender (about 15 minutes). Remove the chervil and parsley and liquidize the mixture in a food blender. Pour into a saucepan and stir in the white sauce and as much milk as is required to achieve the desired consistency. Bring to the boil and season with salt and pepper. Stir in the cream just before serving and reheat almost to boiling point. Pour into a heated tureen and sprinkle with finely chopped parsley or chervil.

Preparation: 10 minutes.
Total time: 35 minutes.

Chicken à la chasseur

1 2¾-lb/1.2-kg chicken, cut into 8 portions
salt
pepper
1 tbsp flour
4/3 tbsp oil
1 anchovy fillet
1 tsp rosemary
½ chilli pepper
½ tbsp chopped parsley
½ oz/10 g dried mushrooms, softened in warm water for 15 minutes
1 clove garlic

Opposite:
Menu 11, page 26

²⁄₃ cup/5 fl oz/150 ml white wine
1½ cups/7 oz/200 g sliced button mushrooms,
sautéed in butter
1 tbsp wine vinegar

Season the chicken portions with salt and pepper, dust with flour and brown gently in the oil. Meanwhile, finely chop and mix together the anchovy fillet, rosemary, chilli pepper, chopped parsley, dried mushrooms and garlic. After browning the chicken for 15 minutes, add the chopped mixture and stir well so that the chicken is well coated with the mixture. Cook the chicken over a gentle heat for a further 20-25 minutes. When the chicken is tender, add the wine and sautéed mushrooms; turn up the heat to reduce the sauce slightly, add the vinegar and transfer to a heated serving dish.

Preparation: 15 minutes.
Total time: 50 minutes.

MENU 18

Palm hearts with vinaigrette dressing
Risotto alla Milanese
Spiced calf's liver
Creamed potatoes or spinach
Rich sponge gâteau

Shopping list

1 1¾-lb/800-g can palm hearts ● 4 3½-oz/100-g slices calf's liver ● 2 oz/50 g beef marrow ● 1 lemon ● 1 tomato ● small bunch parsley ● fresh chervil ● 3¼ lb/1½ kg fresh or 2¼ lb/1 kg frozen spinach or 1 can or packet instant creamed potatoes ● 11 oz/325 g risotto rice ● 9 oz/250 g butter ● 10½ oz/300 g sugar ● 3 eggs ● 1 pint/500 ml milk ● 9 fl oz/250 ml heavy/double cream ● 3 oz/80 g chopped mixed peel ● glacé cherries ● ½ lb/225 g rich sponge cake.

From the store cupboard ● olive oil – vinegar – capers – chives – onion – stock – freshly grated Parmesan cheese – red wine – saffron powder – Dijon mustard – 1 shallot – breadcrumbs – vanilla flavoured confectioners'/icing sugar – nutmeg – flour – sunflower oil – sherry – brandy – tarragon – salt – pepper – garlic.

Work schedule ● Make the gâteau and place in the refrigerator. Mix the vinaigrette. Start the risotto. Prepare the creamed potatoes or spinach. Cook the liver.

Palm hearts with vinaigrette dressing

1 1¾-lb/800-g can palm hearts
small bunch parsley
4 lemon wedges
1 tomato, quartered
²⁄₃ cup/5 fl oz/150 ml vinaigrette dressing

Drain the palm hearts and pat dry with kitchen towels; cut into ½-in/2-cm slices and arrange on a white serviette on a serving platter. Garnish with parsley sprigs and lemon and tomato wedges. Serve the vinaigrette dressing (see recipe below) in a jug or sauceboat.

Preparation: 5 minutes.

Vinaigrette dressing

6/4 tbsp olive oil
2 tbsp wine vinegar
1 tbsp finely chopped capers
½ tsp chopped fresh tarragon or a small pinch dried tarragon
1 tbsp chopped parsley
1 tbsp very finely chopped onion
1 tsp chopped chervil
1 tbsp finely chopped fresh chives
salt
pepper

Place all the ingredients in a small bowl and beat until well blended or liquidize for a few seconds in a blender.

Opposite:
Menu 14, page 29

Spiced calf's liver

4 3¹/₂-oz/100-g slices calf's liver
flour
3/2 tbsp sunflower oil
5 tbsp/3 oz/80 g butter
3/2 tbsp Dijon mustard
1 medium-sized shallot, finely chopped
plenty of finely chopped parsley
¹/₂ clove garlic, finely chopped
salt
pepper
breadcrumbs

Dip the liver in flour but do not salt. Heat the oil and half the butter in a frying pan and brown the liver quickly. Remove from the pan and set aside to cool. Mix the mustard with the chopped shallot, parsley, garlic, salt and pepper and juices from the pan in which the liver was browned. Mix well to form a fairly thick paste and spread over both sides of the liver. Coat with breadcrumbs and sprinkle with the remaining melted butter. Place under a preheated broiler/grill to finish cooking, turning once only.

Preparation: 15 minutes.

Rich sponge gâteau

³/₄ cup/3 oz/80 g chopped mixed peel
2-3 tbsp brandy
¹/₂ lb/225 g rich sponge cake
4/3 tbsp sherry
¹/₂ cup/4 oz/125 g sugar boiled in ¹/₂ cup/ 4 fl oz/
125 ml water to make a syrup
2¹/₄ cups/18 fl oz/500 ml thick custard
1¹/₂ cups/9 fl oz/250 ml heavy/double cream
¹/₂ cup/2 oz/50 g vanilla flavoured confectioners'/
icing sugar
glacé cherries

Chop the mixed peel coarsely and soak in the brandy. Cut the sponge cake into three equal layers and sprinkle with a mixture of the sherry and sugar syrup. Spread the bottom and middle layer thickly with the custard and chopped mixed peel. Sandwich the sponge cake together and refrigerate for as long as possible. Whip the cream and sweeten with the vanilla flavoured sugar; use an icing bag to pipe the cream onto the gâteau, and garnish with glacé cherries.

Preparation: 20 minutes.

Risotto alla milanese

¹/₂ onion, finely sliced
5 tbsp/3 oz/80 g butter
2 tbsp/2 oz/50 g beef marrow
11 oz/325 g risotto rice
¹/₄ cup/2 fl oz/60 ml dry red wine
4¹/₄ cups/1³/₄ pints/1 liter chicken stock
generous pinch saffron powder
4/3 tbsp freshly grated Parmesan cheese

Brown the onion in half the melted butter and beef marrow. Add the rice and stir well. Pour in the red wine and cook until the wine has evaporated. Add half the boiling stock and continue to cook over a brisk heat until the rice has absorbed almost all the liquid. Add the saffron and moisten with a little more stock; continue to add more stock when the rice becomes too dry. Stir only after extra liquid is added. After 15 minutes the rice should be tender but still firm, and the risotto should be quite moist. Remove from the heat, add the freshly grated Parmesan and the remaining butter in small pieces and stir well.

Preparation: 30 minutes.

MENU 19

Philippine chicken salad
Veal cutlets/escalopes with lemon sauce
Artichokes Clamart
Raspberries and cream

Shopping list

¾ lb/350 g cooked chicken breast ● ¾ lb/350 g thinly sliced veal cutlets/escalopes ● 1 can bamboo shoots ● 1 lb/450 g frozen or fresh raspberries ● 1 jar mayonnaise ● 4 artichokes ● 5 oz/150 g celery heart ● 3 lemons ● 1 small lettuce ● small bunch parsley ● 1 small packet frozen peas ● 1 small carton heavy/double cream.

From the store cupboard ● curry powder – Tabasco sauce – Worcestershire sauce – vinegar – 1 egg – butter – sunflower oil – flour – salt – pepper.

Work schedule ● Spoon the raspberries into glass dishes and place in the least cold part of the refrigerator. Prepare the sauce for the chicken salad. Set the artichokes to boil. Finish preparing the chicken salad. Cook the veal cutlets/escalopes.

Philippine chicken salad

2 tbsp sunflower oil
1 tbsp curry powder
2 tbsp vinegar
6/4 tbsp mayonnaise
4 drops Tabasco sauce
6 drops Worcestershire sauce
juice of ½ lemon
¾ lb/350 g cooked chicken breast, cut into strips

5 oz/150 g celery heart, cut into strips
7 oz/200 g bamboo shoots, drained and cut into strips
4 lettuce leaves
1 hard-boiled egg, quartered or sliced
a few sprigs parsley

Heat the oil in a small saucepan, add the curry powder and cook for 2 minutes; add the vinegar and cook until reduced by half; allow to cool before mixing with the mayonnaise, Tabasco and Worcestershire sauces and lemon juice. Pour the mixture over the chicken, celery and bamboo strips and mix thoroughly. Arrange the chicken salad on lettuce leaves on individual side plates and garnish with hard-boiled egg and parsley.

Preparation: 20 minutes.

Veal cutlets/escalopes with lemon sauce

¾ lb/350 g thinly sliced veal cutlets/escalopes
flour
3 tbsp/1½ oz/40 g butter
salt
pepper
3/2 tbsp lemon juice
chopped parsley
thin slices of lemon, rind and pith removed

Place the cutlets/escalopes between two sheets of greaseproof paper and beat until they are very thin. Dip in flour and fry, a few at a time, in a large frying pan in very hot butter. Season each cutlet/escalope as it is cooking, and move to one side of the pan to keep hot while the others are cooking. Once all the cutlets/escalopes are cooked, spread them out in the frying pan and add the lemon juice. Remove from the heat, cover and leave in a warm place for a few minutes. Transfer to a heated serving dish, sprinkle with the chopped parsley and garnish with the slices of lemon.

Preparation: 15 minutes.
Total time: 20 minutes.

Artichokes Clamart

4 artichokes
1 lemon
1 tbsp flour
6 tbsp/3 oz/80 g butter
½ tsp salt
4/3 tbsp cooked peas

Cut off the stalk and the top half of each artichoke. Trim the points of the remaining leaves; open out and pull away the inner middle leaves and remove the choke, leaving a central hollow. Rub the cut surfaces immediately with lemon and place the artichokes in a bowl of acidulated water to prevent discolouration. Mix the flour with a little cold water and pour into a narrow, high-sided saucepan. Add 2½ tbsp/generous 1 oz/30 g butter, salt, 1 tbsp lemon juice, the prepared artichokes and just enough cold water to cover the artichokes. Cook for 15-20 minutes or until the artichokes are just tender. Heat the peas separately in butter.

Arrange the artichokes on a serving platter and fill with the peas.

Preparation: 15 minutes.
Total time: 30 minutes.

MENU 20

Avocados with caviar
Parmentier soup
Trout with almonds
Steamed potatoes
Chocolate gâteau

Shopping list

4 7-oz/200-g trout ● 4 oz/125 g caviar or lumpfish roe ● 2 avocados ● 1 cooking apple ● 2 lemons ● 2 large leeks ● 1 tube mayonnaise ● 1 small carton heavy/double cream ● 1 small carton sour cream ● 9 fl oz/250 ml milk ● 2¼ lb/1 kg new potatoes ● fresh chervil or parsley ● 3 slices bread ● 2 oz/50 g flaked almonds ● 1 chocolate gâteau.

From the store cupboard ● olive oil – flour – stock – butter – freshly grated Parmesan cheese – salt – pepper.

Work schedule ● Start preparation of the Parmentier soup. Prepare the avocados but do not add the caviar (or lumpfish roe); chill in the refrigerator. Set the potatoes to steam. Cook the trout. Finish the Parmentier soup.

Avocados with caviar

2 ripe avocados
1 cooking apple
juice of 1 lemon
3/2 tbsp mayonnaise
1-2 tbsp olive oil
salt
pepper
³⁄₄ cup/4 fl oz/125 ml sour cream
scant ¹⁄₂ cup/4 oz/125 g caviar (or lumpfish roe)

Cut the avocados lengthwise in half. Remove the stones and scoop out the flesh. Place the skins in the refrigerator. Peel and core the apple. Dice the avocado flesh and the apple and sprinkle immediately with half the lemon juice. Beat the mayonnaise lightly with the remaining lemon juice, olive oil, salt and pepper. Pour over the diced avocado and apple and mix carefully. Chill in the refrigerator for at least 40 minutes. Fill the avocado skins with the apple and avocado mixture; place a spoonful of sour

cream on each and top with the caviar (or lumpfish roe) just before serving.

Preparation: 12 minutes.
Refrigeration: 40 minutes.

Parmentier soup

2 leeks, cleaned and thinly sliced
¹⁄₄ cup/2 oz/25 g butter
4¹⁄₄ cups/1³⁄₄ pints/1 liter stock
1 lb/450 g potatoes, peeled
scant 1 cup/7 fl oz/225 ml hot milk
³⁄₄ cup/4 fl oz/125 ml heavy/double cream
pepper
2 tbsp chopped fresh chervil or parsley
freshly grated Parmesan cheese
croûtons

pepper
flour
6 tbsp/3 oz/80 g butter
a few drops lemon juice
scant ¹/₂ cup/2 oz/50 g flaked almonds

Gut and clean the trout, coat with seasoned flour and fry gently in the butter. Remove the skin carefully from one side only and place the fish in a shallow ovenproof dish. Sprinkle with a few drops of lemon juice and the flaked almonds and pour over the butter in which they were cooked. Place under a preheated broiler/grill and serve when the almonds have turned a pale golden brown.

Preparation: 15 minutes.
Total time: 25 minutes.

Steamed potatoes

1¹/₄ lb/600 g new potatoes
salt

The great advantage of this method of cooking is that it is almost impossible to overcook the potatoes and they do not spoil if kept warm for any length of time. Peel and trim the potatoes to a uniform size and shape and place in a steamer over a pan of boiling water. Sprinkle the potatoes with salt and cover with a tightly fitting lid. Steam for 20-30 minutes.

Preparation: 30 minutes.

Gently fry the sliced leeks in the butter, add the stock and the whole potatoes and cook for 45 minutes. Remove the potatoes and mash while still hot; return to the pan and add the hot milk, stirring until the desired consistency is obtained. Before serving, add the cream and freshly ground pepper and bring the soup almost to the boil; remove from the heat and pour into a warmed tureen. Add the chopped fresh chervil. Serve with freshly grated Parmesan cheese and croûtons crisped in the oven, not fried.
If time is short or if leeks are not in season, use canned Parmentier soup; add the cream just before the soup boils and sprinkle with chopped fresh chervil.

Preparation: 15 minutes.
Total time: 1 hour.

Trout with almonds

4 7-oz/200-g trout
salt

MENU 21

**Melon and shrimp/prawns
Polynesian style
Veal chops Provençale
Creamed potatoes
Baked peaches**

Shopping list

1 small melon ● 4 peaches ● 1 9-oz/250-g jar cooked shrimp/prawns ● 1 carton heavy/double cream ● 1 tube mayonnaise ● 4 5-oz/150-g veal loin chops or cutlets (on the bone) ● 1 small lettuce ● small bunch parsley ● 2 large firm ripe tomatoes ● 1 can or packet instant creamed potatoes ● 2 oz/50 g macaroons.

From the store cupboard ● flaked/desiccated coconut – chilli sauce – cayenne pepper – butter – onion – garlic – oil – flour – milk – sugar – salt – pepper.

Work schedule ● Prepare the melon and place in the refrigerator. Prepare the peaches and place in the oven. Cook the veal chops; make the creamed potatoes.

Melon and shrimp/prawns Polynesian style

1 small melon
1 9-oz/250-g jar cooked shrimp/prawns
2 tbsp flaked/desiccated coconut
¹/₂ cup/4 fl oz/125 ml Louis dressing (see recipe above right)

4 lettuce leaves
small bunch parsley

Peel the melon and cut into cubes, discarding the seeds. Place the cubes in a bowl, add the well drained shrimp/prawns, the coconut and the Louis dressing. Mix well. Place a lettuce leaf on each plate and spoon one-quarter of the mixture on to each leaf. Garnish with parsley.

Preparation: 10 minutes.

Louis dressing

1 tbsp heavy/double cream
a few drops chilli sauce
4/3 tbsp mayonnaise
1 tbsp finely chopped onion
pinch cayenne pepper
1 tbsp finely chopped parsley

Place the cream in a bowl and mix in the chilli sauce before stirring in the remaining ingredients. This dressing is delicious with mixed salads.

Veal chops Provençale

4 5-oz/150-g veal loin chops or cutlets (on the bone)
salt
pepper
2 tbsp flour
3/2 tbsp oil
3 tbsp/1½ oz/40 g butter
2 large firm ripe tomatoes
2 tbsp finely chopped onion
1 clove garlic
1 tbsp chopped parsley

Season the chops or cutlets with salt and pepper, coat with flour and fry in oil; when the chops are almost cooked, add the butter. Drain the chops and keep warm between two plates. Peel the tomatoes, remove the seeds and cut into small dice. Fry the onion and garlic in the cooking juices and fat in the pan; when the onion is golden brown, remove the garlic, add the diced tomatoes and parsley and simmer for 5 minutes. Add a little salt and pour the sauce over the veal chops.

Preparation: 15 minutes.

Baked peaches

4 peaches
2 tbsp superfine/caster sugar
¾ cup/2 oz/50 g macaroons
2 tbsp/1 oz/25 g butter

Wash the peaches but do not peel; run a sharp knife all round the stone and cut the peaches in half. Sprinkle each peach half with a little sugar and a spoonful of crumbled macaroons and pour over the melted butter. Bake in a preheated medium oven (350°F/180°C/mk 4) for 15-20 minutes or until the peaches are soft. Serve piping hot.

Preparation: 15 minutes.
Total time: 40 minutes.

MENU 22

Swiss salad
Roman chicken and egg soup
**Entrecôte steaks with pizzaiola
sauce**
Creamed potatoes
Sliced oranges in maraschino

Shopping list

4 7-oz/200-g entrecôte beef steaks ● 7 oz/200 g cooked ham, sliced fairly thickly ● 7 oz/200 g Emmental or Gruyère cheese or processed cheese slices ● 4 oranges ● 1 small jar gherkins ● 1 can or packet instant creamed potatoes ● 1 ripe tomato ● 1 small lettuce ● 1 small bottle vinaigrette or homemade vinaigrette dressing (see p. 34). ● small bunch parsley ● 4 eggs ● 1 7-oz/200-g can tomatoes ● 1 bottle maraschino.

From the store cupboard ● freshly grated Parmesan cheese – salt – nutmeg – pepper – chicken stock – olive oil – sunflower oil – garlic – butter – oregano.

Work schedule ● Make the Swiss salad and place in the refrigerator to chill. Prepare the Sliced oranges in maraschino, cover the bowl and chill in the refrigerator. Heat the chicken stock for the soup. Prepare the creamed potatoes. Cook the steaks; finish and serve the soup.

Swiss salad

7 oz/200 g cooked thick ham slices, cut into strips
7 oz/200 g Emmental, Gruyère or processed cheese slices, cut into strips
2-3 gherkins, cut into strips
1 ripe tomato, seeds removed, cut into strips
1/2 cup/4 fl oz/125 ml vinaigrette dressing (see p. 34)
1 hard-boiled egg, sliced
4 lettuce leaves

Mix all the ingredients together with the exception of the sliced hard-boiled egg and the lettuce leaves. Place a lettuce leaf on each plate and arrange the salad on top. Garnish with slices of hard-boiled egg.

Preparation: 15 minutes.

Roman chicken and egg soup

3 eggs
4/3 tbsp freshly grated Parmesan cheese
1 tbsp finely chopped parsley
pinch grated nutmeg
pinch salt
4 cups/1 1/2 pints/800 ml chicken stock, preferably homemade

Combine the eggs, Parmesan cheese, parsley, nutmeg and salt in a basin and beat with a balloon whisk or fork. Pour this mixture in a thin stream into the boiling chicken stock, stirring with the balloon whisk. Simmer for a further minute or two, stirring occasionally. Serve in consommé dishes.

Preparation: 15 minutes.

Entrecôte steaks with pizzaiola sauce

3/2 tbsp sunflower oil
4 7-oz/200-g entrecôte beef steaks
1 clove garlic, crushed but still in one piece
1 cup/7 oz/200 g canned tomatoes, chopped
salt
pepper
a little butter
pinch oregano
1 tsp chopped parsley

Heat the oil until very hot and add the steaks. Brown both sides to seal (they should still be quite rare); drain and set aside to keep warm

between two hot plates. Sauté the crushed garlic clove briefly in the remaining oil in the pan and then discard. Add the tomatoes and a little salt and pepper and boil for a few minutes until reduced. Lower the heat; add a little butter and a pinch of oregano and simmer very gently for a further 4 minutes. Remove the pan from the heat and place the steaks in the sauce; turn them once or twice in the sauce, then transfer to a heated serving platter. Pour the sauce over the meat and sprinkle with chopped parsley. Serve at once.

Preparation: 15 minutes.

MENU 23

Grapefruit and vodka cocktail
George's rigatoni
Turkey breasts Parisian style
Hazelnut ice cream torte

Shopping list

1 lb/450 g turkey breast, boned ● 3½ oz/100 g prosciutto/raw ham, very thinly sliced with equal proportions of fat and lean ● 2 large ripe grapefruit ● small bunch fresh mint ● small bunch parsley ● 5 oz/150 g freshly grated Parmesan cheese ● 4 eggs ● 14 oz/400 g rigatoni or maniche (large ribbed macaroni) ● 1 7-oz/200-g can sliced cooked button mushrooms ● 1 packet or can mushroom sauce ● 7 fl oz/200 ml light/single cream ● 1 frozen hazelnut ice cream torte.

From the store cupboard ● butter – vodka – cocktail cherries – flour – salt – pepper – sunflower oil – onion – brandy – nutmeg.

Work schedule ● Prepare the grapefruit but do not add the vodka; place in the refrigerator to chill. Start cooking the turkey breasts. Finish the grapefruit. Set out the ingredients for the rigatoni and add the pasta to the boiling water.

Grapefruit and vodka cocktail

(serve in sundae dishes or in special two-tier dishes containing cracked ice)

2 large ripe grapefruit, well chilled
4 tbsp vodka, well chilled
4 cocktail cherries
8 fresh mint leaves

Wash and dry the grapefruit, cut in half and remove any pips. Use a very sharp-pointed knife or a grapefruit knife to loosen each segment; do not detach completely. Shortly before serving, pour 1 tbsp of vodka over each grapefruit half. Garnish with mint leaves and a cocktail cherry and serve in individual dishes.

Preparation: 10 minutes.

George's rigatoni

14 oz/400 g rigatoni or maniche (large ribbed macaroni)
½ cup/3½ fl oz/100 ml light/single cream
3 egg yolks
pinch nutmeg
salt
pepper

6 tbsp/3 oz/80 g butter
3½ oz/100 g prosciutto/raw ham, very thinly sliced with equal proportions of fat and lean, cut into strips

While the pasta is cooking in plenty of boiling salted water, prepare the sauce. Lightly beat together the cream, egg yolks, nutmeg and a little salt and pepper. Melt half the butter over a low heat in a large frying pan. Add the thinly sliced prosciutto/raw ham strips and warm through. When the pasta is tender but still firm, drain well and add to the butter and prosciutto/raw ham in the frying pan; stir for about 1 minute over a low heat. Pour in the egg and cream mixture and dot the remaining butter over the surface. Allow to warm through for a few seconds, until the sauce thickens slightly.

Remove from the heat, add the grated Parmesan, mix well and transfer to a heated serving dish.

Preparation: 20 minutes from the time the pasta is added to the boiling water.

Turkey breasts Parisian style

1 tbsp finely chopped onion
¼ cup/2 oz/50 g butter
1 7-oz/200-g can cooked button mushrooms
5/3 tbsp light/single cream
¾ cup/6 fl oz/175 ml mushroom sauce
1 tsp brandy
1 lb/450 g boned turkey breast, cut into 8 small slices
salt
pepper
2 tbsp flour

1 egg, beaten with:
1 tbsp finely chopped parsley
1 tbsp freshly grated Parmesan cheese
pinch grated nutmeg
3/2 tbsp sunflower oil

Fry the onion in half the butter. Add the sliced mushrooms, the cream and the mushroom sauce; cover the pan and simmer over a low heat for 5 minutes to reduce and thicken the sauce, stirring occasionally. Stir in the brandy. While the sauce is reducing, season the turkey slices with salt and pepper, coat with flour and dip in the egg mixture. Heat the oil in a frying pan and brown the turkey slices on both sides; lower the heat, add the remaining butter and cook over a moderate heat until the turkey is tender. Arrange the turkey slices on a heated serving dish, and cover with the mushroom sauce.

Preparation: 30 minutes.

MENU 24

Baked potatoes with caviar
Tournedos Marquis de Sade
Buttered asparagus tips or artichoke hearts
Coupe Alexandra

Shopping list

4 7-oz/200-g tournedos steaks ● 4 medium baking potatoes of equal size ● 2 oz/50 g unsalted butter ● 1 small carton light/single cream ● 1 small carton sour cream ● ¼ lb/125 g caviar or lumpfish roe ● ½ white loaf of bread ● 1 small jar tomato sauce or paste ● 1 small black truffle (or substitute *cèpes*) ● 1 can asparagus tips or artichoke hearts ● 1 can fruit salad ● 2 oz/50 g fresh or frozen strawberries ● 2 portions strawberry ice cream.

From the store cupboard ● butter – stock – dry sherry – sunflower oil – salt – pepper – kirsch – chives or onion.

Work schedule ● Turn on the oven. Prepare the fruit salad and chill in the refrigerator. Place the potatoes in the oven and put the bread slices in the oven to dry. Cook the asparagus tips or artichoke hearts in butter. Prepare the steaks.

Baked potatoes with caviar

4 medium baking potatoes of equal size
¼ cup/2 oz/50 g unsalted butter
¼ lb/125 g caviar or lumpfish roe
½ cup/4 fl oz/125 g sour cream
3/2 tbsp chopped chives or thinly sliced onion rings

Do not peel the potatoes, simply wash them well and dry thoroughly. Wrap each potato tightly in foil and bake in a hot oven (400°F/200°C/mk 6) for 55 minutes. When the potatoes are cooked, cut lengthwise through the foil and place a generous knob of butter in each. Press the potatoes together again. Serve at once, handing round the caviar or lumpfish roe separately with small dishes of sour cream, chopped chives or onion rings.

Preparation: 5 minutes.
Total time: 55 minutes.

Tournedos Marquis de Sade

4 7-oz/200-g tournedos steaks
¼ cup/2 oz/50 g butter
1 tbsp sunflower oil
salt
pepper
4 thick slices bread (crusts removed), crisped in the oven
1 small black truffle (or substitute cèpes)
½ cup/4 fl oz/125 ml dry sherry
4/3 tbsp stock or water
1 tbsp tomato sauce or paste
4/3 tbsp light/single cream

Brown the steaks in half the butter and 1 tbsp oil. Season with salt and pepper, remove from the frying pan and place on the crisped bread slices. Cover and keep warm. Cut thin slices of truffle, warm gently in the remaining butter and place a slice on top of each steak. Pour the sherry and stock into the frying pan and stir until reduced. Add the remainder of the truffle, cut into fine strips, and the tomato sauce and boil

Coupe Alexandra

2-3 tbsp kirsch
1 can fruit salad
2 portions strawberry ice cream
½ cup/2 oz/50 g fresh or frozen strawberries

Stir the kirsch into the fruit salad and chill in the refrigerator for as long as possible. Just before serving, turn the fruit salad into a chilled crystal bowl (or individual glass dishes); place the ice cream in the center of the fruit (use an ice cream scoop if desired) and garnish with strawberries.

Preparation: 5 minutes.
Refrigeration: 50 minutes.

for 30 seconds; add the cream, heat almost to boiling point and pour over the steaks.

Preparation: 15 minutes.

MENU 25

Gin and grapefruit cocktail
Crêpes Marquise
Quick-fried steaks
Fried artichoke hearts
Apple turnovers

Shopping list

4 grapefruit or 1 1¾-lb/750-g can grapefruit segments ● small bunch mint ● ¾ lb/350 g ripe apples ● 1 can artichoke hearts ● 4 individual beef steaks ● 5 oz/150 g smoked salmon ● 7 fl oz/ 200 ml heavy/double cream ● 2 eggs ● 7 fl oz/200 ml milk or canned cream of celery soup ● 7 oz/200 g frozen puff pastry.

From the store cupboard ● butter – gin – brandy – cocktail cherries – 1 lemon – vanilla flavoured confectioners'/icing sugar – cayenne pepper – sugar – flour – Worcestershire sauce – oil – salt – pepper.

Work schedule ● Prepare the grapefruit cocktail and chill in the refrigerator. Make the pancakes (see p. 30). Cook the apples. Fry the artichoke hearts and finish the pancakes. Make the Apple turnovers and place in the oven. Fry the steaks.

Gin and grapefruit cocktail

(serve in sundae dishes or in special two-tier dishes containing cracked ice)

4 grapefruit, well chilled (or 1 1¾-lb/750-g can grapefruit segments, drained and chilled for as long as possible)
½ cup/4 fl oz/125 ml gin
4 cocktail cherries
8 mint leaves

Peel the grapefruit carefully with a very sharp knife, removing all the pith. Detach each segment and peel off the thin inner skin. Place the segments in individual dishes with any juice from the grapefruit skin, pour over the gin and decorate with cocktail cherries and mint leaves.

Preparation: 15 minutes.

Crêpes Marquise

scant 1 cup/7 fl oz/200 ml white sauce or canned cream of celery soup
1¼ cups/7 fl oz/200 ml heavy/double cream
5 oz/150 g smoked salmon, coarsely chopped

4 drops Worcestershire sauce
a few drops lemon juice
pinch cayenne pepper
4 large or 8 small pancakes (see p. 30)

Mix the white sauce or celery soup with the cream and add 4/3 tbsp to the chopped smoked salmon; stir, then add the Worcestershire sauce, lemon juice and cayenne pepper. Mix well. Spoon an equal quantity of this mixture into the center of each pancake and fold in half, pressing the edges lightly together. Arrange the pancakes, slightly overlapping, in a well-buttered ovenproof dish and cover with the remaining sauce. Cook in a very hot oven (450°F/230°C/mk 8) for 10 minutes.

Preparation (with ready-made pancakes): 25 minutes, otherwise 45 minutes.

Quick-fried steaks

4 individual beef steaks
1 tbsp oil
salt
pepper

Pound the steaks ¹/₁₀ in/2 mm thick with the flat edge of a cleaver blade or meat bat. Brush each steak lightly on both sides with oil. Cook very briefly over a high heat, season with salt and pepper and serve without delay.

Preparation: 15 minutes.

Apple turnovers

³/₄ lb/350 g ripe apples
2 tbsp/1 oz/25 g butter
¹/₄ cup/2 oz/50 g sugar
1 tbsp brandy
7 oz/200 g frozen puff pastry, thawed
1 egg
vanilla flavoured confectioners'/icing sugar

Peel, core and slice the apples. Melt the butter in a heavy-bottomed frying pan, add the apples and fry briefly. Add the sugar and the brandy and mix carefully; remove from the heat and allow to cool. Roll out the pastry ¹/₄ in/5 mm thick and cut out circles 4 in/10 cm in diameter. Place 1 tbsp of cooked apples in the center of each circle, moisten the edges with a little water and fold over into a semicircle; pinch the edges together gently to seal. Brush with beaten egg, prick each turnover with a fork and bake in a preheated hot oven (400°F/200°C/mk 6) for 10-12 minutes. A couple of minutes before they are cooked, sprinkle with confectioners'/icing sugar and bake for two minutes to caramelize the sugar. Serve very hot.

Preparation: 20 minutes.
Total time: 35 minutes.

MENU 26

Andalusian gazpacho
Turkey slices in Marsala sauce
Creamed potatoes or peas with
butter
Cassata ice cream dessert

Shopping list

1¼ lb/600 g turkey breast, boned ● 1 cucumber ● 1 onion ● 2 medium-sized peppers, preferably 1 green and 1 yellow ● 3 large ripe tomatoes ● small bunch parsley ● 2¼ lb/1 kg fresh peas or 1 can or packet instant creamed potatoes ● 1 small sliced loaf ● 1 frozen cassata ice cream dessert.

From the store cupboard ● butter – fresh breadcrumbs – garlic – olive oil – vinegar – flour – Marsala, Madeira or sherry – stock – 1 lemon – salt – pepper – sunflower oil – chilli pepper.

Work schedule ● Make the Andalusian gazpacho and chill in the refrigerator. Prepare the creamed potatoes or cook the peas with butter. Cook the turkey slices.

Andalusian gazpacho

⅓ cup/1 oz/25 g fresh breadcrumbs
1 cucumber
1 small onion
2 medium-sized peppers, preferably 1 green and 1 yellow
3 large ripe tomatoes
½ clove garlic
4/3 tbsp olive oil
4/3 tbsp wine vinegar
small piece chilli pepper, finely chopped
10 ice cubes
salt
pepper

2 slices white bread
3/2 tbsp finely chopped parsley

Soak the breadcrumbs in a little water. Trim and wash all the vegetables, setting aside small quantities of pepper and cucumber which will be diced and served as garnishes with the croûtons and chopped parsley. Squeeze excess moisture from the soaked breadcrumbs and place in a liquidizer or food processor with the vegetables, garlic, oil, vinegar, chilli pepper and ice cubes. Liquidize until smooth and well blended, season with salt and pepper and add a little iced water if the soup is too thick. Place in the refrigerator to chill. Serve in a chilled soup tureen. Serve diced cucumber, peppers, croûtons and chopped parsley separately.

Preparation: 10 minutes.
Total time: 1 hour.

Turkey slices in Marsala sauce

1¼ lb/600 g turkey breast, boned and cut into 8 slices
salt
pepper
2 tbsp flour
3/2 tbsp sunflower oil
3 tbsp/1½ oz/40 g butter
⅓ cup/2½ fl oz/75 ml Marsala, Madeira or sherry
⅓ cup/2½ fl oz/75 ml hot chicken stock
a few drops lemon juice

Season the turkey slices with salt and pepper, coat with flour and brown lightly on both sides in hot oil. Lower the heat, add the butter and cook over a moderate heat. When the turkey slices are tender, pour in the Marsala and turn the turkey several times to absorb the flavour; remove from the heat and place the well drained slices on a heated serving platter. Cover with another hot plate. Add the hot stock to the juices in the pan and boil rapidly until the sauce has reduced by half, add a few drops of lemon juice and pour over the turkey slices.

Preparation: 15 minutes.

MENU 27

Cheese choux puffs
Chinese fondue
Coffee cream gâteau

Shopping list

1¾ lb/800 g fillet or sirloin of beef ● 10½ oz/300 g shin of beef or stewing cut for making stock in the pressure cooker ● 1 beef bone for the stock ● 1 stick celery, 1 carrot and 1 onion for the stock ● 4 eggs ● 3½ oz/100 g freshly grated Parmesan cheese ● 18 fl oz/500 ml milk ● at least 4 of the following sauces: mayonnaise, vinaigrette, soy sauce, tartare sauce, sauce diable (devil sauce), tomato ketchup ● 1 coffee gâteau.

From the store cupboard ● butter – flour – salt – tomato ketchup.

Work schedule ● Trim and dice the meat. Make 3¼ cups/1½ pints/800 ml beef stock in the pressure cooker. Set out a selection of sauces. Make the choux puffs; while they are baking, make the cheese sauce filling.

Cheese choux puffs

¾ cup/6 fl oz/175 ml cold water
pinch salt
3 tbsp/1½ oz/40 g butter
½ cup + 4 tbsp/2¾ oz/75 g flour
2 whole eggs + 1 egg yolk, plus 1 extra egg for glazing
generous 1 cup/9 fl oz/250 ml thick cheese sauce (see recipe right)

Place the water, salt and butter in a small saucepan and bring to a fast boil; pour the flour into the saucepan all at once. Remove from the heat immediately and beat with a wooden spoon. Stir continuously until all the flour is absorbed and the mixture is smooth and comes away cleanly from the sides of the saucepan. Transfer to a basin, allow to cool slightly and beat in the eggs one at a time. Grease a sheet of foil with butter and place on a baking sheet. Use an icing bag to pipe out 20 small choux balls. Brush with beaten egg and bake at 400°F/200°C/mk 6 for 20 minutes or until golden and well risen. Remove from the oven, slit each puff and use an icing bag to fill the buns with the hot cheese sauce.

Preparation: 10 minutes.
Total time: 35 minutes.

Cheese sauce

Make generous 1 cup/9 fl oz/250 ml thick white sauce, stir in 4/3 generous tbsp freshly grated Parmesan cheese and simmer for 10-12 minutes.

Chinese fondue

1¾ lb/800 g fillet or sirloin of beef
3¾ cups/1½ pints/800 ml beef stock made in a pressure cooker
At least 4 of the following sauces arranged in individual bowls for each guest: mayonnaise, vinaigrette, soy sauce, tartare sauce, sauce diable (devil sauce), tomato ketchup.

Prepare the meat as for Fondue bourguignonne (see p. 22) and cook the meat in the hot stock in the same way. In China the beef stock is also drunk when the meat is finished. It is therefore a good idea to provide each guest with a consommé cup and to have a ladle ready.

Preparation: 10 minutes.

MENU 28

Spaghetti with compressed smoked roe
Ham salad
Vanilla ice cream with hot chocolate sauce

Shopping list

7 oz/200 g cooked ham ● 1 jar mayonnaise ● 5 fl oz/150 ml virgin olive oil ● 5 oz/150 g *botargo* (smoked mullet roe) or smoked cod's roe ● 14 oz/400 g spaghetti ● small bunch parsley ● 1 head white celery ● 1 cos lettuce ● 2 cooking apples ● 4 oz/125 g plain chocolate ● 1 block vanilla ice cream.

From the store cupboard ● milk – butter – Tabasco or chilli sauce – Dijon mustard – mustard powder – 1 lemon.

Work schedule ● Prepare the salad and mix the dressing. This should be poured over the salad at the last minute, just before serving. Grate the smoked roe. Cook the spaghetti. Make the chocolate sauce (see p.129) and keep it warm until needed.

Spaghetti with compressed smoked roe

5 oz/150 g botargo (smoked mullet roe) or smoked cod's roe
14 oz/400 g spaghetti
½ cup/4 fl oz/125 ml virgin olive oil
3/2 tbsp chopped parsley

Grate the smoked roe finely. A special Parmesan cheese grater is useful for this job. When the spaghetti is nearly cooked, place the olive oil and the grated roe in a small saucepan and heat gently; the grated roe must not fry. When the spaghetti is *al dente* (tender but still firm), drain and place in a heated tureen; add the warm *botargo* dressing, stir carefully and sprinkle with chopped parsley. Serve at once.

Preparation: 20 minutes.

Ham salad

1 tsp Dijon mustard
½ tsp mustard powder
juice of ½ lemon
10 drops Tabasco or chilli sauce
5/3 tbsp mayonnaise
3/2 tbsp olive oil
7 oz/200 g cooked ham, sliced thickly and cut into strips
1 celery heart, cut into strips
1 cos lettuce
2 cooking apples, diced

Mix the Dijon mustard and mustard powder with the lemon juice; add the Tabasco or chilli sauce, the mayonnaise and oil. Blend thoroughly; just before serving pour over the salad and mix well.

Preparation: 10 minutes.

MENU 29

Asparagus Milan style
Baked porgy/sea bream or bass
Mixed salad with oil and lemon dressing
Strawberries Romanoff

Shopping list

1 3-lb/1.3-kg porgy/sea bream or bass ● 3¼ lb/1½ kg fresh asparagus ● 1 lb/450 g fresh strawberries ● 4 eggs ● 3½ oz/100 g freshly grated Parmesan cheese ● mixed salad ingredients ● 1 sprig rosemary ● small bunch parsley ● 3 lemons ● 1 orange ● 1 small carton heavy/double cream.

From the store cupboard ● butter – chilli pepper – white wine – Worcestershire sauce – vanilla flavoured confectioners'/icing sugar – flour – sunflower oil – olive oil – garlic – Curaçao – salt – pepper.

Work schedule ● Mix the strawberries with the orange juice and Curaçao and place in the refrigerator to chill. Prepare the fish. Cook the

asparagus. Prepare the salad. Whip the cream. Finish the asparagus.

Asparagus Milan style

3¼ lb/1½ kg fresh asparagus, washed and trimmed
4 eggs
½ cup + 2 tbsp/5 oz/150 g butter
scant ½ cup/3½ oz/100 g freshly grated Parmesan cheese
salt
pepper

Steam the asparagus for 10-15 minutes or until tender. Fry the eggs in a little butter, seasoning lightly with salt and pepper (avoid the yolks). Arrange the asparagus in 4 neat bundles on a heated serving plate, the tips pointing towards the center. Sprinkle the tips with freshly grated Parmesan and plenty of hot butter to melt the cheese. Place a fried egg in the spaces in between or on top of the asparagus. Serve at once with extra hot melted butter.

Preparation (once the asparagus is cooked): 10 minutes.
Total time: 40 minutes.

Baked porgy/sea bream or bass

1 3-lb/1.3-kg porgy/sea bream or bass
salt
pepper
2-3 tbsp lemon juice
10 drops Worcestershire sauce
1 clove garlic
1 sprig rosemary
small piece chilli pepper
2 tbsp flour
4/3 tbsp sunflower oil
½ cup/4 fl oz/125 ml dry white wine
½ cup/2 oz/50 g butter
small bunch parsley
4 lemon wedges

Gut and wash the fish and season inside and out with salt, pepper, lemon juice and 10 drops Worcestershire sauce; put the garlic, rosemary and chopped chilli pepper inside the fish. Coat lightly with flour and place in an ovenproof dish containing 4/3 tbsp oil. Bake at 350°F/180°C/mk 4 for 30-35 minutes; turn the fish after 15 minutes. When the fish is cooked, pour over the wine and leave in the oven with the heat turned off for a further 15 minutes. Transfer to a heated serving platter, pour over the cooking juices and noisette butter (melted and cooked until it turns a light golden brown) and garnish with sprigs of parsley and lemon wedges.

Preparation: 10 minutes.
Total time: 50 minutes.

Strawberries Romanoff

1 lb/450 g fresh strawberries
juice of 1 orange
2 tbsp Curaçao
1 cup/5 fl oz/150 ml heavy/double cream
½ cup/2 oz/50 g vanilla flavoured confectioners'/icing sugar

Rinse, drain and hull the strawberries. Mix with the orange juice and Curaçao and chill in the refrigerator. Whip the cream and sweeten with the vanilla flavoured confectioners'/icing sugar. Partially drain the strawberries and serve in individual glass sundae dishes or a large crystal bowl. Decorate with the whipped cream.

Preparation: 10 minutes.
Refrigeration: 1 hour.

Smoked sturgeon with brown
bread and butter
Consommé à la reine
Bitoks (Russian veal patties)
with asparagus tips
Pancakes Cevennes style

Shopping list

¾ lb/350 g smoked sturgeon ● 1 loaf brown bread ● 1 large can consommé ● 1 small packet frozen choux balls (or see p. 48) ● 14 oz/400 g finely ground/minced lean veal ● 18 fl oz/500 ml milk ● 2½ oz/60 g cooked lean ham ● 3 eggs ● 1 small carton light/single cream ● 1 can asparagus tips ● 7 oz/200 g marrons glacés.

From the store cupboard ● fresh breadcrumbs – flour – clarified butter (see p. 11) – nutmeg – butter – rum – sugar – salt – pepper.

Work schedule ● Make the pancakes (see p. 30). Make the veal patties. Finish the pancakes and set aside, ready to be placed in the oven. Finish cooking the veal patties and the asparagus.

Consommé à la reine

1 large can good quality consommé (4 servings)
½ packet frozen choux balls for garnish (or homemade choux balls – see p. 48)

Make the choux balls. Heat the consommé according to the instructions on the can. Pour into heated consommé cups or bowls and serve the choux balls separately.

Preparation: 5 minutes.
Total time: 20 minutes.

Bitoks (Russian veal patties) with asparagus tips

1¾ cups/14 oz/400 g finely ground/minced lean veal
2½ oz/60 g lean cooked ham, finely chopped
1⅓ cups/4 oz/125 g fresh white breadcrumbs, soaked in milk and squeezed free of excess
2 egg yolks
nutmeg
salt
pepper
2 tbsp flour
3/2 tbsp clarified butter
5/3 tbsp light/single cream
1 can asparagus tips

Mix the veal, ham, soaked breadcrumbs and egg yolks in a bowl with a pinch of nutmeg, salt and pepper. Shape into 4 flat, oval patties. Coat lightly with flour and fry in clarified butter. Drain and keep warm between two hot plates. Add a little salt and pepper and the cream to the pan. Boil for a few minutes to thicken, then reduce the heat, add the asparagus tips and heat briefly. Arrange the veal patties on a heated serving platter with a few asparagus tips on top of each patty. Cover with the sauce and serve.

Preparation: 20 minutes.

Pancakes Cevennes style

7 oz/200 g marrons glacés
¼ cup/2 fl oz/60 ml rum
8 pancakes (see p. 30)
2 tbsp sugar

Chop the marrons glacés into small pieces and sprinkle with the rum. Place a little of this mixture inside each pancake, roll up and place

Opposite:
Menu 17, page 33

in a lightly buttered ovenproof dish; dredge with sugar and place in a fairly hot preheated oven (375°F/190°C/mk 5) to caramelize the surface.

Preparation (with ready-made pancakes): 15 minutes, otherwise 35 minutes.

MENU 31

Pancakes with Emmental cheese
Veal chops/cutlets Milanese
Roast potatoes
Salad with thousand island dressing
Raspberries Melba

Shopping list

5 eggs • 12 slices Emmental cheese • 7 oz/200 g lean cooked ham, thinly sliced • 1 small carton heavy/double cream • 4 7-oz/200-g veal chops/cutlets, on the bone • 1 lemon • 1 jar mayonnaise • small bunch parsley • 2¼ lb/1 kg potatoes • 1 cos lettuce • 10½ oz/300 g fresh or frozen raspberries • 1 oz/ 25 g almonds • 1 small bottle Melba sauce • 1 small carton whipping cream • 9 fl oz/250 ml milk • 10½ oz/300 g vanilla ice cream.

From the store cupboard • nutmeg – breadcrumbs – butter – sunflower oil – chilli sauce – onion – Grand Marnier – vanilla flavoured confectioners'/icing sugar – salt – pepper – mustard powder – paprika.

Work schedule • Pour the Grand Marnier over the raspberries and chill in the refrigerator. Make the pancakes, fill with the cheese stuffing and place in an ovenproof dish. Start cooking the potatoes. Prepare the thousand island dressing. Wash and drain the salad. Place the pancakes in the oven. Cook the veal.

Pancakes with Emmental cheese

12 slices Emmental cheese
7 oz/200 g lean cooked ham, thinly sliced
8 pancakes (see p. 30)
nutmeg
paprika
⅔ cup/5 fl oz/150 ml heavy/double cream

Place a slice of cheese and a small slice of ham on each pancake; season with nutmeg and paprika. Fold both sides of the pancake over towards the center and then roll up the pancake. Arrange in a buttered ovenproof dish, pour over the cream and place half a slice of Emmental on each pancake roll. Bake in a preheated oven at 450°F/230°C/mk 8 for 10 minutes.

Preparation (with ready-made pancakes): 10 minutes, otherwise 45 minutes.

Veal chops/cutlets Milanese

4 7-oz/200-g veal chops/cutlets, on the bone
1 egg
3/2 tbsp breadcrumbs
4/3 tbsp sunflower oil
3 tbsp/1½ oz/40 g butter
salt
lemon

Wipe the meat with a dry cloth to remove any bone splinters; pound lightly with a meat bat and make a series of small cuts along the edges. Dip in unsalted beaten egg and coat with breadcrumbs. Fry the chops/cutlets in very hot oil and butter until well browned. Once both sides are browned, lower the heat and cook until tender. Remove from the pan, drain, salt lightly and set aside between two hot plates. Leave for 5 minutes before serving. Transfer to a heated serving dish and garnish with lemon wedges.

Preparation: 15 minutes.

Opposite:
Menu 18, page 34

Thousand island dressing

4/3 tbsp mayonnaise
1 level tbsp finely chopped onion
1 chopped hard-boiled egg
pinch mustard powder
1/2 tsp chilli sauce
1 tsp finely chopped parsley

Mix all the ingredients thoroughly and pour over the mixed salad.

Raspberries Melba

1 tbsp Grand Marnier
2 cups/10 1/2 oz/300 g fresh or frozen raspberries
1 3/4 cups/10 1/2 oz/300 g vanilla ice cream
6/4 tbsp Melba sauce
4/3 tbsp whipped cream, sweetened with vanilla flavoured confectioners'/icing sugar
1 tbsp toasted flaked almonds

Pour the Grand Marnier over the raspberries and chill in the refrigerator. Place individual sundae glasses in the refrigerator to chill. Just before serving, place a scoop of ice cream in each glass and top with the raspberries. Pour over the Melba sauce and decorate with the whipped cream and toasted flaked almonds.

Preparation: 10 minutes.

MENU 32

Smoked eel with fried egg
Meat kebabs with oriental pilaf rice
Mixed salad
Fresh fruit

Shopping list

1/2 loaf brown bread ● 7 oz/200 g long grain rice ● 4 eggs ● 1 oz/25 g seedless white raisins/sultanas ● 1 oz/25 g pine nuts ● 3/4 lb/350 g smoked filleted eel ● a selection of fresh fruit ● 1 lettuce or mixed salad ingredients ● 4 small grilling tomatoes (optional) ● 2 ripe tomatoes (or canned) ● 2 onions ● small bunch parsley ● 7 oz/200 g lean beef ● 7 oz/200 g lean veal ● 7 oz/200 g lean pork ● 1 can sweet peppers ● 1 bottle barbecue sauce.

From the store cupboard ● butter – Worcestershire sauce – 1 lemon – paprika – soy sauce – sunflower oil – vinegar – chilli pepper – bay leaves – salt – pepper – Tabasco sauce – stock.

Work schedule ● Marinate the cubes of meat. Wash and drain the salad. Trim the smoked eel and cut into thick slices. Start the pilaf rice. Prepare the kebabs. Fry the eggs.

Smoked eel with fried egg

4 slices brown bread
2 1/2 tbsp/1 1/2 oz/40 g butter
4 eggs, fried
3/4 lb/350 g smoked filleted eel, cut into thick slices
8 wafer-thin onion rings
small bunch parsley

Toast and butter the bread, place one fried egg on each slice and arrange the smoked eel slices on top. Garnish with the onion rings and sprigs of parsley.

Preparation: 15 minutes.

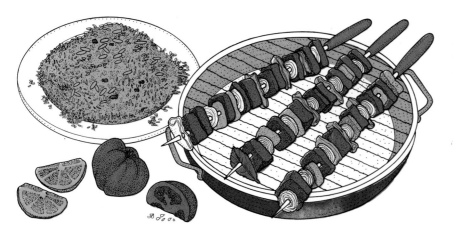

juice, paprika, soy sauce, salt and pepper. Mix well and marinate for as long as possible. Cut the pepper into 1-in/2.5-cm squares. Peel the onion and detach and parboil the larger outer layers in salted water; cut into 1-in/2.5-cm squares. Spear the various ingredients on skewers, alternating the different types of meat, the onion and pepper. Heat the oil in a large frying pan until very hot and brown the kebabs on all sides; lower the heat, add the butter and continue cooking, turning every few minutes until the meat is tender. Arrange the kebabs on a bed of pilaf rice. Pour over the cooking juices and garnish with the broiled/grilled tomatoes. Serve barbecue sauce separately in a sauceboat.

Preparation: 40-50 minutes.

Oriental pilaf rice

1 tbsp chopped onion
3 tbsp/1½ oz/40 g butter
1 cup/7 oz/200 g long grain rice
3/2 tbsp drained diced tomato flesh, seeds removed
½ chilli pepper, crumbled
1 canned red pepper
¼ cup/1 oz/25 g seedless white raisins/sultanas, softened in lukewarm water
¼ cup/1 oz/25 g pine nuts
½ bay leaf
1¼ cups/½ pint/300 ml hot stock

Brown the onion in the butter in an ovenproof casserole; add the rice and cook for 1 minute. Add the tomato, chilli pepper, red pepper, seedless white raisins/sultanas, pine nuts and bay leaf and mix well. Pour in the hot stock, bring to the boil, cover and place in a preheated oven at 350°F/180°C/mk 4 for 18 minutes. Do not stir or remove the lid during cooking. Transfer the rice to a heated serving dish and stir gently with two forks to separate the grains.

Preparation: 10 minutes.
Total time: 30 minutes.

Meat kebabs with oriental pilaf rice

7 oz/200 g lean beef, cut into 1-in/2.5-cm cubes
7 oz/200g lean veal, cut into 1-in/2.5-cm cubes
7 oz/200 g lean pork, cut into 1-in/2.5-cm cubes
10 drops Worcestershire sauce
6 drops Tabasco sauce
juice of ½ lemon
1 tbsp paprika
1 tbsp soy sauce
salt
pepper
1 large canned sweet pepper
1 large onion
3/2 tbsp sunflower oil
2½ tbsp/1½ oz/40 g butter
4 portions oriental pilaf rice (see recipe right)
4 small broiled/grilled tomatoes (optional)
barbecue sauce (optional)

Place the meat in a large bowl and sprinkle with Worcestershire sauce, Tabasco sauce, lemon

---

MENU 33

Turtle soup
Omelette soufflée with peas
George's scampi kebabs
Pilaf rice
Chestnut cream gâteau

Shopping list

1 can turtle soup (4 servings) ● 2¼ lb/1 kg frozen or 4½ lb/2 kg fresh scampi or Dublin Bay prawns ● 6 eggs ● 1 small packet frozen peas ● 1 slice streaky bacon, ½ in/1 cm thick ● 12 salad tomatoes (optional) ● lemon balm ● 1 small cos lettuce ● ½ pint/300 ml heavy/double cream ● 10½ oz/300 g marrons glacés ● 1 chocolate sponge cake ● 1 small bottle vinaigrette (or homemade – see p. 34) ● chives ● tarragon ● capers.

From the store cupboard ● sunflower oil – rice –

onion – vanilla flavoured confectioners'/icing sugar – sugar – rum – salt – pepper – bay leaves.

Work schedule ● Prepare the Chestnut cream gâteau and chill in the refrigerator. Mix the vinaigrette (see p. 34). Start the pilaf rice (see p. 29). Prepare the scampi kebabs. Heat the Turtle soup. Place the Omelette soufflée in the oven and cook the peas.

Omelette soufflée with peas

6 eggs
salt
pepper
6 tbsp/3 oz/80 g butter
1 small packet frozen peas
a few lettuce leaves
a few thin slices of onion
pinch sugar

Separate the eggs and beat the yolks with the salt and pepper. Whisk the whites until stiff and fold in the yolk mixture gradually, using a metal spoon. Place half the butter in a frying pan. When the butter is very hot, pour in the omelette mixture, heaping it up towards the center. Cook over a moderate heat until golden brown underneath. Make a cut in the center of the omelette and lift up the edges. Continue cooking under a preheated broiler/grill until the omelette is browned on top and firm to the touch. Cook the peas and sauté the onion briefly in the remaining butter; add the lettuce cut into strips, the peas and a pinch of sugar and season with salt and pepper. When the omelette is golden brown fill with this mixture and serve without delay.

Preparation: 5 minutes.
Total time: 25 minutes.

George's scampi kebabs

12 salad tomatoes (optional)
1 slice streaky bacon, ½ in/1 cm thick
2¼ lb/1 kg frozen or 4½ lb/2 kg fresh scampi or Dublin Bay prawns, peeled
lemon balm
bay leaves
2 tbsp sunflower oil
4 portions pilaf rice (see p. 29)
vinaigrette dressing (see p. 34)

Thread the ingredients on to the skewers in the following suggested order: tomato, bacon, scampi, lemon balm, bay leaf. Continue until the skewer is full; thread three tomatoes on to each skewer, at the beginning, in the center and at the end. Brush lightly with oil and broil/grill. Place on a bed of pilaf rice and serve vinaigrette dressing separately.

Preparation: 10 minutes.
Total time: 20 minutes.

Chestnut cream gâteau

1¾ cup/½ pint/300 ml heavy/double cream
½ cup/2 oz/50 g vanilla flavoured confectioners'/icing sugar
1 chocolate sponge cake
2-3 tbsp rum
10½ oz/300 g marrons glacés, chopped

Whip the cream and sweeten with the vanilla flavoured confectioners'/icing sugar. Cut the sponge cake in half, sprinkle with rum and fill with half the cream and the chopped marrons glacés. Cover with the top layer of the cake and decorate with the remaining sweetened whipped cream.

Preparation: 10 minutes.

MENU 34

Snails bourguignonne (Burgundy style)
Veal cutlets/escalopes with Madeira sauce
Cauliflower cheese
Apricot fritters with brandy sauce

Shopping list

2 dozen prepared snails (these can be bought from many delicatessens with the cleaned, purged snails in a can and their shells in a net bag) ● 1 lb/450 g veal cutlets/escalopes ● 1 cauliflower ● 18 fl oz/500 ml milk ● 3 eggs ● 1 small carton heavy/double cream ● 8 fresh apricots or 1 2¼-lb/1-kg can apricots.

From the store cupboard ● butter -- Madeira, Marsala or dry sherry – flour – sugar – confectioners'/icing sugar – brandy – oil for frying – freshly grated Parmesan – salt – pepper.

Work schedule ● Steam the cauliflower and make a white sauce. Pound the cutlets/escalopes with a meat bat. Place the cauliflower cheese in the oven to brown. Prepare the apricot fritters. Cook the cutlets/escalopes and heat the snails according to the manufacturer's instructions. Make the brandy sauce.

Snails bourguignonne (Burgundy style)

2 dozen prepared snails (see shopping list)

Prepare and heat the snails according to the manufacturer's instructions. Serve very hot. If special snail picks and pincer holders are not available, use cake forks or cocktail sticks to remove the snails from their shells.

Preparation: 10-15 minutes.

Veal cutlets/escalopes with Madeira sauce

1 lb/450 g veal cutlets/escalopes
2 tbsp flour
3 tbsp/1½ oz/40 g butter
4/3 tbsp Madeira, Marsala or dry sherry
salt
pepper
1 tbsp stock or water

Pound the cutlets/escalopes between two sheets of greaseproof paper until very thin. Coat lightly with flour, shake off the excess and fry in hot butter in a large frying pan; season with salt and pepper and turn almost immediately. Pour the Madeira into the pan, turn the cutlets/escalopes, cover the pan and turn off the heat. Leave to stand for 4-5 minutes; add 1 tbsp stock or water and heat very briefly. Transfer to a heated serving dish and serve without delay.

Preparation: 15 minutes.

Apricot fritters with brandy sauce

8 fresh apricots or 1 2¼-lb/1-kg can apricots
batter for frying (see p. 33)
oil for frying
confectioners'/icing sugar

Cut the apricots in half and discard the stone; if canned fruit is used, drain well and dry with paper towels. Dip each apricot half in batter and deep fry in hot oil for 5-7 minutes. Arrange on a heated serving dish, sprinkle with confectioners'/icing sugar and serve at once with the brandy sauce.

Preparation: 10 minutes.

Brandy sauce

2 egg yolks
⅔ cup/4 fl oz/125 ml heavy/double cream
1 tsp sugar
6/4 tbsp quality brandy

Place all the ingredients in a small saucepan or ceramic basin and cook gently in a bain marie for 10 minutes, stirring continuously with a wooden spoon or balloon whisk.

Preparation: 10 minutes.

MENU 35

Maryland crab salad
Calf's liver Berlin style
Creamed potatoes
Peaches Sobieski

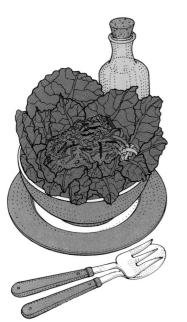

Shopping list

8 2-oz/50-g thin slices calf's liver • 1 7-oz/200-g can crabmeat • 1 14-oz/400-g can sweetcorn • 1 7-oz/200-g can sweet peppers (preferably yellow and red) • 1 can or packet instant creamed potatoes • 1 2¼-lb/1-kg can peaches • 2 onions • 2 green apples • small bunch parsley • 18 fl oz/500 ml milk • 18 fl oz/500 ml heavy/double cream • 1 large tomato • 1 jar redcurrant jelly • 7 oz/200 g raspberry or strawberry ice cream.

From the store cupboard • butter – flour – vanilla flavoured confectioners'/icing sugar – olive oil – 1 lemon – salt – pepper.

Work schedule • Prepare the crab salad and chill in the refrigerator. Set out the ingredients for the Peaches Sobieski. Make the creamed potatoes. Cook the liver.

Maryland crab salad

1 7-oz/200-g can crabmeat
1 14-oz/400-g can sweetcorn
1 7-oz/200-g can sweet peppers (preferably
yellow and red), finely diced
1 tbsp chopped onion
1 tbsp chopped parsley
juice of ½ lemon
3/2 tbsp olive oil
salt
pepper

1 tomato, quartered
small bunch parsley

Place the flaked crabmeat in a bowl with the sweetcorn and finely diced peppers. Add the onion and parsley and dress with a mixture of lemon juice, oil, salt and pepper. Transfer to a deep serving dish and garnish with tomato quarters and sprigs of parsley.

Preparation: 15 minutes.

Calf's liver Berlin style

1 large onion, sliced into thin rings
scant ½ cup/3½ oz/100 g butter
salt
2 crisp green apples, peeled, cored and cut into
thick slices
8 2-oz/50-g thin slices calf's liver
2 tbsp flour
pepper
1 tbsp chopped parsley

Sauté the onion rings in 2 tbsp/1 oz/25 g butter until lightly coloured; sprinkle with salt. Gently fry the apples in a separate frying pan in 2 tbsp/1 oz/25 g butter; turn half way through cooking. While the apples are frying, coat the liver in flour and fry very briefly in the remaining butter. Season with salt and pepper and transfer

immediately to a heated serving dish. Cover with slices of apple and onion rings. Sprinkle with chopped parsley and serve without delay.

Preparation: 20 minutes.

Peaches Sobieski

3 cups/18 fl oz/500 ml heavy/double cream
½ cup/2 oz/50 g vanilla flavoured confectioners'/icing sugar
1 cup/7 oz/200 g raspberry or strawberry ice cream
8 canned peach halves, drained
3/2 tbsp redcurrant jelly

Whip the cream until stiff and fold in the vanilla flavoured sugar. Place a scoop of ice cream in each sundae glass and top with two peach halves and the melted redcurrant jelly. Decorate with whipped cream and serve without delay.

Preparation: 10 minutes.

MENU 36

Avocado with mustard vinaigrette
Cream of chicken soup
Wiener Schnitzel
Green salad
Apple strudel

Shopping list

4 avocados ● 1 cos lettuce ● 1 cabbage lettuce ● 1 lemon ● 1 can cream of chicken soup (4 servings) ● 4 3½-oz/100-g veal cutlets/escalopes ● 2 eggs ● 2 oz/50 g capers ● 1 small can anchovy fillets ● 1 ready-made apple strudel.

From the store cupboard ● breadcrumbs – olive oil – vinegar – butter – Dijon mustard – mustard powder – flour – sunflower oil – salt – pepper.

Work schedule ● Mix the mustard vinaigrette. Hard-boil the egg. Wash the lettuces and prepare the avocados. Cook the Wiener Schnitzel and heat the cream of chicken soup.

Avocado with mustard vinaigrette

4 avocados
½ lemon
4 leaves cos lettuce
3/2 tbsp olive oil
1 tbsp vinegar
1 tbsp Dijon mustard
pinch mustard powder
salt
pepper

Cut the avocados in half and discard the stones. Make criss-cross incisions in the flesh and rub with lemon to prevent discolouration. Arrange the avocado halves on lettuce leaves on individual plates. Mix the vinaigrette: beat together in a bowl the oil, vinegar, French and English mustards, salt and pepper. Pour over the avocados and serve immediately.

Preparation: 10 minutes.

Wiener Schnitzel

4 3½-oz/100-g veal cutlets/escalopes, ¼ in/
½ cm thick
2 tbsp flour
1 egg, beaten
fine breadcrumbs
3 tbsp/1½ oz/40 g butter
4/3 tbsp sunflower oil
salt
1 hard-boiled egg
4 anchovy fillets

4 thin slices lemon, peel and pith removed
1 tbsp capers

Coat the meat in flour; dip in beaten egg, then in breadcrumbs and fry in the hot butter and oil until golden brown on both sides. Remove from the pan and salt lightly. Garnish each cutlet/ escalope with a slice of hard-boiled egg with a rolled up anchovy in the center, a slice of lemon and a few capers.

Preparation: 20 minutes.

MENU 37

Cauliflower and rice mould
Sole meunière
Steamed potatoes
Mixed salad
Rum babas

Shopping list

14 oz/400 g sole fillets ● 1 cauliflower ● 1¾ pints/1 liter milk ● 3½ oz/100 g freshly grated Parmesan cheese ● 1 onion ● 1 lemon ● small bunch parsley ● 2¼ lb/1 kg new potatoes ● mixed salad ingredients ● 1 large or 4 individual rum babas

From the store cupboard ● butter – rice – flour – breadcrumbs – salt – pepper – oil – vinegar.

Work schedule ● Make the white sauce. Sauté the onion in butter. Cook the cauliflower and boil the rice. Start steaming the potatoes. Complete the Cauliflower and rice mould and place in the oven. Soak the fish in milk. Wash and drain the salad. Cook the sole fillets.

Cauliflower and rice mould

3 cups/1¼ pints/750 ml white sauce
4/3 tbsp finely chopped onion
generous ¼ cup/2½ oz/70 g butter
8/5 tbsp risotto rice
salt
pepper
1 medium-sized cauliflower
2 tbsp breadcrumbs
6/4 tbsp freshly grated Parmesan cheese

Make the white sauce. Sauté the chopped onion in half the butter. Meanwhile, boil the rice in salted water for 8-9 minutes; drain and add to the onion and butter; season with salt and pepper. Divide the cauliflower into florets and cook until tender but still quite firm. Butter a shallow ovenproof dish and sprinkle with 1 tbsp breadcrumbs. Arrange the cauliflower in the bottom of the dish and cover with the rice. Sprinkle with Parmesan cheese and cover evenly with white sauce. Dot the surface with butter and sprinkle with the remaining breadcrumbs. Bake in a preheated oven at 350°F/180°C/mk 4 for 15-20 minutes or until the top is golden brown.

Preparation: 20 minutes.
Total time: 40 minutes.

Sole meunière

14 oz/400 g sole fillets
generous 1 cup/9 fl oz/250 ml milk
flour
¼ cup/2 oz/50 g butter
salt

pepper
1 lemon, quartered
small bunch parsley

Soak the fillets of sole in the cold milk for 10 minutes; drain on paper towels, pat dry and coat with flour, Fry gently in butter until pale golden brown. Season lightly with salt and pepper as they are cooking. Arrange the fillets on a heated serving platter and garnish with lemon wedges and sprigs of parsley.

Preparation: 20 minutes.

MENU 38

Shrimp/prawns with mayonnaise
Oxtail consommé
Chicken Picasso
Creamed potatoes
Chocolate gâteau

Shopping list

1 8-oz/225-g jar cooked shrimp/prawns ● 1 small jar mayonnaise ● 2 1½-lb/700-g chickens ● 1 can oxtail consommé (4 servings) ● 1 small lettuce ● 1 lemon ● 1 10½-oz/300-g can tomatoes ● 3½ oz/100 g black olives ● 3½ oz/100 g green olives ● 1 can or packet instant creamed potatoes ● 1 chocolate gâteau.

From the store cupboard ● sunflower oil – butter – salt – pepper.

Work schedule ● Prepare the chickens and place in the oven. Prepare the Shrimp/prawns with mayonnaise. Heat the soup and make the creamed potatoes. Finish the Chicken Picasso.

Shrimp/prawns with mayonnaise

1 8-oz/225-g jar cooked shrimp/prawns
4 lettuce leaves
1 small jar mayonnaise
4 lemon wedges

Drain and dry the shrimp/prawns. Place a lettuce leaf in each of four glass dishes and fill each with one-quarter of the shrimp/prawns. Top with a spoonful of mayonnaise and a lemon wedge. Serve extra mayonnaise separately.

Preparation: 5 minutes.

Chicken Picasso

2 1½-lb/700-g chickens
4/3 tbsp sunflower oil
salt
pepper
1½ cups/10½ oz/300 g tomatoes, skinned, seeded and coarsely chopped
20 green olives, pitted and cut in half
20 black olives, pitted and cut in half

Cut each chicken lengthwise in half. Flatten each half, brush with oil and season with salt and pepper. Roast in a preheated oven at 350°F/ 180°C/mk 4 for 45 minutes. Drain and keep warm. Heat the tomatoes briefly in the juices in the roasting pan; add the olives and cook for a further 5 minutes. Place the chicken halves on a large serving platter and cover with the sauce.

Preparation: 10 minutes.
Total time: 1 hour.

MENU 39

Potted shrimps (served with hot toast and butter)
Rognons Robert
Pilaf rice
Aphrodite salad
Hazelnut ice cream dessert

Shopping list

1 8-oz/225-g jar potted shrimps ● 1 brown loaf ● 2 calf's kidneys ● 1 lemon ● small bunch parsley ● 2 green apples ● 1 celery heart ● 1 small carton natural yogurt ● 10½ oz/300 g long grain rice ● 1 hazelnut ice cream dessert.

From the store cupboard ● butter – brandy – clarified butter (see p. 11) – salt – pepper (black and white) – stock – onion.

Work schedule ● Start the pilaf rice (see p. 29). Prepare the Aphrodite salad. Cook the kidneys. Turn the potted shrimps into a bowl and make the toast.

Rognons Robert

2 calf's kidneys, trimmed, skinned and membrane removed
⅓ cup/2½ oz/70 g clarified butter
2 tbsp brandy
salt
pepper
lemon juice
chopped parsley

Sauté the whole calf's kidneys briskly for no more than three minutes in the very hot clarified butter. Remove the kidneys, pour the brandy into the hot butter and cook until it has evaporated. Slice the kidneys thickly and return to the pan to finish cooking. Season with salt and pepper and add a little lemon juice and chopped parsley. Serve with 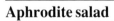 pilaf rice.

Preparation: 15 minutes.

Aphrodite salad

2 green apples
1 celery heart
⅔ cup/5 fl oz/150 ml natural yogurt
salt
black pepper

Peel and core the apples; cut into quarters and slice thinly. Cut the celery heart into 1¼-in/3-cm strips and slice thinly across the grain. Mix with the yogurt, seasoned with a little salt and plenty of freshly ground black pepper.

Preparation: 10 minutes.

MENU 40

Spaghetti with cheese and pepper
Saltimbocca alla salvia (veal, ham and sage rolls)
Zucchini/courgettes with garlic and parsley
Fruit salad with maraschino and vanilla ice cream

Shopping list

14 oz/400 g veal cutlets/escalopes, thinly sliced • 3½ oz/100 g prosciutto/raw ham, thinly sliced • 14 oz/400 g spaghetti • ¼ lb/125 g Pecorino cheese • fresh sage leaves • 1 lb/450 g zucchini/courgettes • small bunch parsley • 1 can fruit salad • ½ lb/225 g vanilla ice cream.

From the store cupboard • butter – maraschino – white wine – stock – flour – garlic – sunflower oil – salt – black and white pepper.

Work schedule • Flavour the fruit salad with maraschino and chill in the refrigerator. Prepare the veal rolls. Slice the zucchini/courgettes. Put the spaghetti on to cook in plenty of boiling salted water. Cook the veal and ham rolls.

Spaghetti with cheese and pepper

14 oz/400 g spaghetti
¼ lb/125 g freshly grated Pecorino cheese
plenty of black pepper, coarsely ground or crushed in a mortar with a pestle
salt

Cook the spaghetti until tender but still firm; drain and place in a heated serving dish. Add the grated Pecorino cheese, black pepper and 3/2 tbsp of the cooking water. Mix thoroughly and serve without delay.

Preparation: 15 minutes.

Saltimbocca alla salvia (veal, ham and sage rolls)

14 oz/400 g veal cutlets/escalopes, thinly sliced
fresh sage leaves
3½ oz/100 g prosciutto/raw ham, thinly sliced
salt
pepper
2 tbsp flour
¼ cup/2 oz/50 g butter
4/3 tbsp white wine
4/3 tbsp light stock

Pound the veal slices until very thin. Place half a sage leaf and a slice of prosciutto/raw ham in the center of each slice; season with salt and pepper and roll up tightly. Thread on to skewers (two or three to a skewer), coat lightly with flour and fry briskly in hot butter until well browned. Pour the white wine and stock into the frying pan and cook over a high heat for a couple of minutes to reduce the sauce. Pour over the veal rolls and serve immediately.

Preparation: 20 minutes.
Total time: 25 minutes.

Zucchini/courgettes with garlic and parsley

1 lb/450 g firm zucchini/courgettes
2 cloves garlic
1½ tbsp/scant 1 oz/20 g butter
2 tbsp oil
salt
pepper
3/2 tbsp chopped parsley

Wash the zucchini/courgettes well, dry and slice very thinly, using a mandoline cutter or a food processor. Sauté the whole garlic cloves in butter and oil; remove and discard. Add the zucchini/courgettes to the pan and sauté for a few minutes (they should remain slightly crisp). Season with salt and pepper just before serving and sprinkle with chopped parsley.

Preparation: 10 minutes.

MENU 41

Risotto with Gorgonzola cheese
Entrecôte steaks with piquant sauce
Jacket potatoes
Mixed salad
Ice cream with whisky

Shopping list

14 oz/400 g risotto rice ● 4 8-oz/225-g boneless loin/entrecôte steaks ● 5 oz/150 g strong Gorgonzola cheese ● 3½ oz/100 g freshly grated Parmesan cheese ● small bunch parsley ● 1 lemon ● 1 small carton light/single cream ● 4 medium-sized baking potatoes ● mixed salad ingredients ● 4 portions vanilla ice cream.

From the store cupboard ● butter – stock – 1 onion – dry white wine – shallots – salt – pepper – tomato ketchup – Worcestershire sauce – hot paprika – clarified butter (see p. 11) – whisky.

Work schedule ● Wash and drain the salad. Put the potatoes in the oven to bake. Start cooking the risotto. Cook the steaks or prepare ingredients and utensils to cook them at the table.

Risotto with Gorgonzola cheese

1 tbsp chopped onion
6 tbsp/3 oz/80 g butter
2 cups/14 oz/400 g risotto rice
generous 1 cup/9 fl oz/250 ml dry white wine
4½ cups/1¾ pints/1 liter chicken stock
5 oz/150 g strong Gorgonzola cheese
2 tbsp freshly grated Parmesan cheese
1 tbsp chopped parsley

Sauté the onion gently in 2½ tbsp/generous 1 oz/30 g butter in a heavy-bottomed frying pan. pan. Add the rice and sauté for a few minutes.

Pour in the white wine and continue cooking until it has evaporated; add half the hot stock and cook for a further 16-18 minutes, adding more stock a little at a time when the rice has absorbed most of the liquid. When the rice is tender but still firm, remove from the heat, add the remaining butter and the Gorgonzola cheese, both cut into small pieces, the grated Parmesan cheese and the chopped parsley. Stir well, using a wooden spatula. Serve without delay.

Preparation: 30 minutes.

Entrecôte steaks with piquant sauce

4 8-oz/225-g loin/entrecôte steaks
salt
½ tsp hot paprika
4/3 tbsp clarified butter (see p. 11)
1 tbsp chopped shallot, or onion with a little garlic
6/4 tbsp white wine
2 tbsp lemon juice
4/3 tbsp light/single cream
1 tsp tomato ketchup
1 tsp Worcestershire sauce

Season the steaks with salt and paprika and brown on both sides in very hot clarified butter. Drain and keep warm between two hot plates. Add the chopped shallot or onion and garlic to the cooking juices in the pan; sauté briefly, add the wine and allow to reduce a little. Add the

lemon juice, cream, tomato ketchup and Worcestershire sauce and cook over a low heat until well blended. Place the steaks on a heated serving platter and cover with the sauce.

Preparation: 15 minutes.

MENU 42

Potato and tomato soup
Crispy chicken breasts
French-fried potatoes
Mixed salad
Banana and orange fruit salad
with kirsch

Shopping list

4 ¼-lb/125-g chicken breasts ● 1½ lb/700 g potatoes ● 1 7-oz/200-g can tomatoes ● 1 large onion ● 3½ oz/100 g freshly grated Parmesan cheese ● ½ white loaf of bread ● 1 packet cornflakes ● 1 small carton natural yogurt ● 1 lemon ● mixed salad ingredients ● 1 packet ready-to-cook French-fried potatoes ● 2 bananas ● 2 oranges.

From the store cupboard ● stock – butter – salt – pepper – oil for frying – kirsch – sugar.

Work schedule ● Start cooking the soup. Marinate the chicken breasts in the yogurt. Wash and drain the salad. Place the croûtons in the oven to crisp. Prepare the fruit salad and chill in the refrigerator. Put the chicken breasts in the oven. Fry the potatoes.

Potato and tomato soup

1 large onion
1½ lb/700 g potatoes peeled and diced
6 tbsp/3 oz/80 g butter
1 cup/7 oz/200 g tomatoes, sieved
6 cups/2½ pints/1½ liters homemade stock
salt
pepper
plenty of freshly grated Parmesan cheese
2 thick slices of white bread, cut into cubes

Sauté the onion and the diced potatoes gently in three-quarters of the butter. Do not allow to brown. Add the tomatoes and cook for 5 minutes. Pour in the hot stock, season with salt and pepper and cook until the potatoes are tender. While the soup is cooking, place the croûtons in the oven to crisp. Remove the soup from the heat, allow to cool slightly, then liquidize in a blender. Add plenty of freshly grated Parmesan cheese. Just before serving, sauté the croûtons very briefly in the remaining butter, sprinkle with grated Parmesan cheese and serve on a separate plate.

Preparation: 40 minutes.

Crispy chicken breasts

4 ¹⁄₄-lb/125-g chicken breasts, boned
4 tbsp crushed cornflakes
²⁄₃ cup/5 fl oz/150 ml natural yogurt
¹⁄₄ cup/2 oz/50 g butter
salt
4 lemon wedges

Flatten the chicken breasts and leave to marin-ate in the yogurt for 30-35 minutes. Drain the chicken breasts and coat with crushed corn-flakes, pressing the flakes well on to the chicken. Place in a buttered ovenproof dish, sprinkle with a little salt and melted butter and broil/grill for 15 minutes, turning twice, until tender inside and crunchy on the outside. Transfer to a heated serving platter and garnish with lemon wedges.

Preparation: 55 minutes.

MENU 43

Chilled avocado soup
Fried chicken with lemon and herbs
Mixed salad
Pears flamed in rum

Shopping list

2 1½-lb/700-g oven-ready chickens ● 3 avocados ● 1 small carton natural yogurt ● 1 small carton light/single cream ● 1 lemon ● ½ white loaf of bread ● 1 small ripe tomato ● 1 onion ● small bunch parsley ● rosemary ● 1 2¼-lb/1-kg can pears ● mixed salad ingredients.

From the store cupboard ● butter – Worcester-shire sauce – Tabasco sauce – salt – pepper – olive oil – wine vinegar – rum.

Work schedule ● Start cooking the chickens. Make the avocado soup and chill in the re-frigerator. Wash and drain the salad. Warm the pears gently in the juice from the can.

Chilled avocado soup

3 large ripe avocados
a few drops lemon juice
²⁄₃ cup/5 fl oz/150 ml natural yogurt
6/4 tbsp light/single cream
5 ice cubes
4 drops Worcestershire sauce
4 drops Tabasco sauce
salt
pepper
1 small ripe tomato, diced
3/2 tbsp finely chopped onion
3/2 tbsp chopped parsley
2 thick slices bread, cut into cubes and crisped in the oven

Peel the avocados and remove the stones; reserve half an avocado (sprinkle with lemon juice to prevent discoloration). Liquidize the avocado flesh in a blender with the yogurt, cream, ice cubes, Worcestershire sauce, Tabas-co, a few drops of lemon juice and a little salt and pepper; if the soup is too thick add a little cold water. Refrigerate until required. Serve in consommé cups and garnish with the diced half avocado, the diced tomato, chopped onion and parsley and the croûtons.

Preparation: 10 minutes.
Refrigeration: 50 minutes.

Fried chicken with lemon and herbs

2 1½-lb/700-g oven-ready chickens
3 tbsp/1½ oz/40 g butter
2 sprigs rosemary, chopped and mixed with salt and pepper
2 tbsp olive oil
juice of ½ lemon

Cut the chicken along the breast bone and press flat. Sprinkle with the chopped rosemary, salt and pepper. Butter two large heavy frying pans; place a chicken in each pan, inside facing down, and dot the remaining butter over the surface of the birds. Cover with greaseproof paper and then with a tightly fitting lid. Fry over a very low heat for 30 minutes; turn the chickens and continue to cook for a further 30 minutes. Remove from the heat; beat the olive oil and the lemon juice and pour into the frying pans. Turn the chickens in this liquid, cover and leave to stand for 5 minutes before serving.

Preparation: 10 minutes.
Total time: 1 hour.

Pears flamed in rum

1 2¼-lb/1-kg can pears
½ cup/4 fl oz/125 ml rum

Warm the pears gently in the juice from the can. Remove from the juice with a slotted spoon and place, rounded side uppermost, on a very hot serving dish. Heat the rum in a small saucepan, set alight and pour the flaming spirit over the pears; shake the dish gently to allow the rum to burn more freely.

Preparation: 10 minutes.

MENU 44

Country soup with croûtons
Paprika pork chops with sauerkraut
Creamed potatoes
Apple pie

¾ lb/350 g frozen mixed vegetables • 4 5-oz/150-g pork chops • 4 oz/125 g Parmesan cheese • ½ white loaf of bread • 1 small carton sour cream • 1 1½-lb/700-g can sauerkraut • 1 can or packet instant creamed potatoes • 9 fl oz/250 ml milk • 1 ready-made apple pie.

From the store cupboard • butter – stock – clarified butter (see p. 11) – flour – onion – dry white wine – meat extract/essence – salt – pepper – paprika.

Work schedule • Start preparing the Country soup. Crisp the croûtons in the oven. Start frying the pork chops. Make the creamed potatoes.

Country soup with croûtons

¾ lb/350 g frozen mixed vegetables
6 cups/2½ pints/1½ liters stock
a little butter
½ cup/4 oz/125 g freshly grated Parmesan cheese
slices of bread, cut into cubes, crisped in the oven

Stir the frozen vegetables into the cold stock; bring to the boil and simmer (see instructions on the packet for cooking time). Remove from the heat, add a small piece of butter and stir in half the grated Parmesan cheese; serve the remaining cheese and the croûtons separately.

Preparation: 10 minutes.

Paprika pork chops with sauerkraut

4 5-oz/150-g pork chops
salt

pepper
2 tbsp flour
¼ cup/2 oz/50 g clarified butter
½ tbsp finely chopped onion
1 tbsp paprika
⅔ cup/5 fl oz/150 ml dry white wine
1 tsp meat extract/essence, diluted in hot water
⅔ cup/5 fl oz/150 ml sour cream
1 1½-lb/700-g can sauerkraut

Season the pork chops with salt and pepper, coat lightly with flour and fry in the clarified butter. When tender, remove from the frying pan, drain and keep warm between two hot plates. Cook the onion in the meat juices until pale golden brown; add the paprika and cook for a further 2 minutes; pour in the white wine and allow to evaporate. Add the diluted meat extract/essence and the sour cream and boil gently, until the sauce has thickened. Meanwhile, heat the sauerkraut; drain and transfer to a serving dish. Arrange the pork chops on top and serve the sauce separately in a jug or sauceboat.

Preparation: 15 minutes.
Total time: 30 minutes.

MENU 45

Ribbon noodles with prosciutto/ raw ham
Veal rissoles with pizzaiola sauce
Creamed potatoes
Dubliner (ice cream, coffee and whiskey dessert)

14 oz/400 g ground/minced lean veal • 1 lb/450 g tagliolini (ribbon noodles), preferably fresh • 3½ oz/100 g prosciutto/ raw ham, very thinly sliced with equal proportions of fat and lean • 4 oz/125 g freshly grated Parmesan cheese • 1 egg • ½ white loaf of bread • 5 fl oz/150 ml milk • small bunch parsley • 1 anchovy fillet • 9 oz/250 g canned tomatoes • 1 bay leaf • 1 small carton whipping cream • 1 can or packet instant creamed potatoes • 2 portions vanilla ice cream.

From the store cupboard • butter – Irish whiskey – coffee – nutmeg – oregano – chilli peppers – garlic – onion – sunflower oil – salt – pepper – bay leaf.

Opposite:
Menu 26, page 47

Work schedule ● Whip the cream. Make and cook the rissoles. Cook the ribbon noodles.

Ribbon noodles with prosciutto/raw ham

1 lb/450 g tagliolini (ribbon noodles), preferably fresh
3½ oz/100 g prosciutto/raw ham, very thinly sliced, with equal proportions of fat and lean
scant ½ cup/3 oz/80 g butter
freshly ground pepper
pinch salt
½ cup/4 oz/125 g freshly grated Parmesan cheese

Add the noodles to a large pan of boiling salted water. While they are cooking, warm the prosciutto/raw ham (cut into thin strips) in a large frying pan, using all the butter. When the noodles are tender but still firm, drain, turn into the frying pan with the ham and butter and stir briefly over a low heat. Add pepper, a little salt and half the Parmesan cheese. Serve the remaining Parmesan cheese separately.

Preparation: 10 minutes.

Veal rissoles with pizzaiola sauce

⅔ cup/5 fl oz/150 ml boiling milk
2 slices bread, crusts removed
1¾ cups/14 oz/400 g ground/minced lean veal
1 egg
1 tbsp freshly grated Parmesan cheese
1 tbsp finely chopped parsley
salt
pinch nutmeg
6/4 tbsp sunflower oil
1 tbsp finely chopped onion
a mixture of the following ingredients, finely chopped:
  1 clove garlic
  1 anchovy fillet
  ½ chilli pepper
  sprig parsley
1 bay leaf
1⅓ cups/9 oz/250 g canned tomatoes
1 tsp oregano

Pour the boiling milk on to the bread and leave to stand; squeeze to remove the excess and place the softened bread in a bowl with the veal, egg, grated Parmesan cheese, parsley, salt and nutmeg. Mix well and shape into rissoles. Heat half the oil in a large frying pan and brown the rissoles briskly on both sides. Do not cook right through; remove from the pan, drain and keep warm between two plates. Add the remaining oil to the pan and brown the onion; add the chopped mixture of garlic, anchovy, chilli pepper and parsley, together with the bay leaf and tomatoes. Cook over a moderate heat for 15 minutes; discard the bay leaf and return the rissoles to the frying pan to finish cooking. After a further 10-15 minutes, add the oregano. Serve with creamed potatoes.

Preparation: 40 minutes.

Opposite:
Menu 35, page 62

Dubliner (ice cream, coffee and whiskey dessert)

2 portions vanilla ice cream
4 cups strong black coffee
4 tbsp Irish whiskey
⅔ cup/5 fl oz/150 ml whipping cream

Whip the cream but do not sweeten. Place a small scoop of ice cream in each of 4 tall glasses; pour in the coffee and the whiskey and top with the whipped cream.

Preparation: 10 minutes.

MENU 46

Melon and port cocktail
Spaghetti with bacon
and Parmesan cheese
Breaded chicken drumsticks
Salad with remoulade sauce
Omelette soufflée au Grand Marnier

Shopping list

4 chicken legs, on the bone ● 1 large or 2 small melons ● small bunch mint ● 2 lemons ● 14 oz/400 g spaghetti ● 9 eggs ● 5 oz/150 g smoked streaky bacon ● 4 oz/125 g freshly grated Parmesan cheese ● 14 fl oz/400 ml mayonnaise ● 2 oz/50 g capers ● small bunch parsley ● chervil ● 1 orange.

From the store cupboard ● butter – cocktail cherries – ruby port – sugar – vanilla flavoured confectioners'/icing sugar – milk – sunflower oil – salt – pepper – chives – Grand Marnier – breadcrumbs.

Work schedule ● Prepare the melon and chill in the refrigerator. Shape the chicken legs (see method) and marinate. Make the remoulade sauce; wash and drain the salad. Start cooking the spaghetti. Fry the chicken legs. Place the Omelette in the oven.

Melon and port cocktail

1 large or 2 small melons
juice of ½ lemon
sugar

½ cup/4 fl oz/125 ml ruby port
4 cocktail cherries
4 leaves fresh mint

Peel the melon; discard the seeds and cut the flesh into ½-in/1-cm cubes. Sprinkle with the lemon juice, stir and chill in the refrigerator for at least 45 minutes. Moisten the rim of 4 wide glasses with water and dip in sugar; fill with the diced melon, pour a little port into each glass and decorate with cocktail cherries and mint.

Preparation: 10 minutes.
Refrigeration: 45 minutes.

Spaghetti with bacon and Parmesan cheese

14 oz/400 g spaghetti
⅔ cup/5 oz/150 g smoked streaky bacon, diced
1 tbsp sunflower oil
2 large eggs
4/3 tbsp freshly grated Parmesan cheese
1½ tbsp cold milk
1½ tbsp/scant 1 oz/20 g melted butter
salt
pepper

While the spaghetti is boiling in plenty of salted water, sauté the bacon in the oil. Place the eggs, Parmesan cheese, milk, melted butter, salt and pepper in a bowl and beat well. When the spaghetti is tender but still firm, drain and add to the frying pan with the bacon and oil. Stir over a low heat for a few seconds and then pour in the egg and cheese mixture; when the sauce has thickened slightly, remove from the heat and serve.

Preparation: 30 minutes.

Breaded chicken drumsticks

4 chicken legs on the bone, skinned
1 egg and a little milk

breadcrumbs
4/3 tbsp oil
3 tbsp/1½ oz/40 g butter
salt
1 lemon, cut into wedges
small bunch parsley

Slit the chicken thighs lengthwise through to the bone and work the flesh from the bone with the aid of a sharp knife. The drumstick bone is retained. Trim away any tendons and turn the flesh inside out. Once most of the drumstick bone is exposed, pound the attached chicken flesh with a meat bat. Beat the egg with a little cold milk and soak the chicken portions in this mixture. Drain, coat liberally with breadcrumbs and fry in the hot oil and butter. When the chicken is cooked, remove from the pan, drain and place on a heated serving platter. Sprinkle with a little salt. Garnish with lemon wedges and sprigs of parsley.

Preparation: 45 minutes.

Remoulade sauce

1¾ cups/14 fl oz/400 ml mayonnaise
1 hard-boiled egg, finely chopped
1 tbsp chopped capers
1 tsp chopped chives
1 tsp chopped parsley
1 tsp chopped fresh chervil

Mix all the above ingredients together, pour over the salad just before serving.

Omelette soufflée au Grand Marnier

3 egg yolks
¼ cup/2 oz/50 g granulated sugar
pinch salt
finely grated peel of ½ orange
5 egg whites
vanilla flavoured confectioners'/icing sugar
generous ¼ cup/2½ fl oz/70 ml Grand Marnier

Place the egg yolks, granulated sugar, salt and orange peel in a bowl and beat thoroughly. Whisk the egg whites and fold in the yolk and sugar mixture. Heat an ovenproof dish with a little sugar sprinkled in the bottom and fill with the soufflé mixture, heaping it slightly and making a slit in the center. Sprinkle with a little more sugar and place in a preheated oven at 350°F/180°C/mk 4 for 20-25 minutes or until the top is golden brown. Sprinkle a little vanilla flavoured confectioners'/icing sugar around the edges of the dish. Heat the Grand Marnier, pour over the omelette soufflée and flame.

Preparation: 10 minutes.
Total time: 35 minutes.

MENU 47

Minestrone soup
Pork chops Bavarian style
Steamed potatoes
Fresh fruit

Shopping list

4 5-oz/150-g pork chops ● ¾ lb/350 g frozen mixed vegetables ● 2¼ lb/1 kg new potatoes ● 2 large potatoes (or rice or small pasta shapes) ● 1 onion ● 1 14-oz/400-g can tomatoes ● 4 oz/125 g freshly grated Parmesan cheese ● bunch fresh basil ● 2 Cox's or Reinette apples ● 1 small jar redcurrant jelly ● 1 1½-lb/700-g can cooked red cabbage ● small bunch parsley ● 1 lemon ● selection of fresh fruit.

From the store cupboard ● oil – flour – stock – salt – pepper.

Work schedule ● Start cooking the Minestrone soup. Prepare the potatoes for steaming (see p. 40). Cook the pork chops and heat the red cabbage.

Minestrone soup

1 tbsp finely chopped onion
3/2 tbsp oil
2 cups/14 oz/400 g canned tomatoes, sieved
6 cups/2½ pints/1½ liters stock, preferably home-made
¾ lb/350 g frozen mixed vegetables
2 potatoes, peeled (or rice or small pasta shapes)
fresh basil, chopped and mixed with ½ cup/4 oz/125 g freshly grated Parmesan cheese

Sauté the onion gently in the oil; add the sieved tomatoes and heat through, stirring once or twice. Combine this mixture with the stock and

juice of 1 lemon
1 1½-lb/700-g can cooked red cabbage
4 5-oz/150-g pork chops
pepper
2 tbsp flour
3/2 tbsp sunflower oil
4/3 tbsp redcurrant jelly
4 sprigs parsley

Cut the apples in half but do not peel; carefully remove the core to leave a hollow in the middle of each apple half. Place in a small saucepan, cover with cold water and add a pinch of salt and the lemon juice. Bring to the boil and remove from the heat immediately. While the red cabbage is heating in a heavy-bottomed casserole, season the pork chops with salt and pepper, coat with flour and fry in oil in a large frying pan; drain the chops, arrange on a heated serving platter and place half an apple (the hollow filled with redcurrant jelly) on top of each chop. Surround with red cabbage and garnish with sprigs of parsley.

Preparation: 25 minutes.

frozen vegetables. Add the potatoes or rice or pasta shapes, bring to the boil and simmer for 25-30 minutes. Mash the potatoes (if used) into the soup to thicken. Remove the saucepan from the heat and sprinkle in half the freshly grated Parmesan cheese and chopped basil. Serve the remaining cheese separately.

Preparation: 10 minutes.
Total time: 45 minutes.

Pork chops Bavarian style

2 Cox's or Reinette apples
pinch salt

MENU 48

**Cream of artichoke and
pea soup
Palm hearts with Parmesan and
hot butter dressing
Trout baked in red wine**
Mixed salad
Crêpes Suzette

Shopping list

4 7-oz/200-g trout ● 1 can cream of pea soup (2 servings) ● 1 can cream of artichoke soup (2 servings) ● 1 small can artichoke hearts ● 1 small carton light/single cream ● 1 large can palm hearts ● 4 oz/125 g freshly grated Parmesan cheese ● 1 carrot ● 1 onion ● thyme ● bay leaf ● small bunch parsley ● mixed salad ingredients ● 1 lemon ● 1 egg ● 9 fl oz/250 ml milk ● 5 oz/150 g superfine/caster sugar ● 2 oranges.

From the store cupboard ● Armagnac or brandy – Grand Marnier – Dijon mustard – oil – wine vinegar – meat extract/essence – dry red wine – flour – salt – pepper.

Work schedule ● Make the pancakes (see p. 30). Wash and drain the salad. Start cooking the trout. Sauté the artichoke hearts in butter. Heat the palm hearts and the soup.

Cream of artichoke and pea soup

1 small can artichoke hearts
2 tbsp/1 oz/25 g butter
salt
pepper
1 small can cream of pea soup (2 servings)
1 small can cream of artichoke soup (2 servings)
6/4 tbsp light/single cream

Slice the artichoke hearts and heat in their own juice. Sauté lightly in the butter and season with salt and pepper. Mix the soups together and heat; just before serving, stir in the cream. Reheat the soup but do not allow to boil. Pour into a heated tureen and add the sliced artichoke hearts.

Preparation: 10 minutes.
Total time: 20 minutes.

Palm hearts with Parmesan and hot butter dressing

1 large can palm hearts
plenty of freshly grated Parmesan cheese
generous ¹/₂ cup/5 oz/150 g melted butter, seasoned with freshly ground pepper and a little salt

Heat the palm hearts according to the manufacturer's instructions. Drain, dry and cut in half.

Arrange on a heated serving dish and sprinkle liberally with grated Parmesan cheese and very hot melted butter.

Preparation: 15 minutes.

Trout baked in red wine

4 7-oz/200-g trout
salt
pepper
¹/₂ carrot, thinly sliced
1 tbsp finely chopped onion
¹/₂ cup + 2 tbsp/5 oz/150 g butter
bouquet garni: bay leaf, thyme and parsley, tied together in a piece of muslin
2¹/₄ cups/18 fl oz/500 ml light dry red wine
1 tsp flour
¹/₂ tsp meat extract/essence, dissolved in 1 tbsp hot water

Season the gutted trout inside and out with salt and pepper. Sauté the sliced carrot and onion in a little butter. Butter an ovenproof casserole, arrange the fish head to tail and add the bouquet garni and red wine; the fish should be just covered by the wine. Bring to the boil over direct heat and then bake in a preheated oven at 350°F/180°C/mk 4 for 10-12 minutes. Remove the trout carefully and keep warm on a serving platter covered with foil. Strain the cooking liquid through a fine sieve and boil hard to

reduce by half; add a *beurre manié* (work the flour together with 2 tbsp/1 oz/25 g butter and drop into the liquid). Add the diluted meat extract/essence; boil gently for 2-3 minutes. Remove from the heat, stir in a few more flakes of butter and pour the sauce over the fish. Serve without delay.

Preparation: 20 minutes.
Total time: 35 minutes.

Crêpes Suzette
(can be prepared at the table)

piece orange peel
piece lemon peel
scant ½ cup/3 oz/80 g superfine/caster sugar
2 tbsp/1 oz/25 g butter
6/4 tbsp orange juice
2 tbsp lemon juice

3/2 tbsp Grand Marnier
8 pancakes (see p. 30)
generous ¼ cup/2½ fl oz/70 ml Armagnac or brandy

Place the orange and lemon peel, three-quarters of the sugar and the butter in a frying pan. Spear the orange and lemon peel with the prongs of a fork and stir the sugar until it dissolves. Add the orange and lemon juice and heat until the sauce thickens slightly. Add the Grand Marnier, boil for a further minute. Add the first pancake, moisten with the sauce, dust lightly with sugar and fold into quarters. Move to one side of the pan and repeat the process with the remaining pancakes. Pour in the Armagnac, heat gently, set alight and flame.

Preparation (with ready-made pancakes): 10 minutes, otherwise 30 minutes.

MENU 49

Savoury tuna toasts
Chicken Calcutta
Pilaf rice
Cream caramel

Shopping list

1 2¾-lb/1.2-kg chicken ● 1 white loaf of bread ● ¾ lb/350 g canned tuna ● 1 tube mayonnaise ● 1 lettuce ● 1 lemon ● 1 large salad tomato ● 2 oz/50 g capers ● 1 egg ● 1 onion ● 1 small carton natural yogurt ● 2 large ripe tomatoes or 1 small can tomato paste ● 1 fresh ginger root or ground ginger ● 1 small carton light/single cream ● 1 packet instant cream caramel (4 servings) ● 7 oz/200 g long grain rice
● Ingredients for "sambals" (see p. 28): 1 banana ● 2 oz/50 g seedless white raisins/sultanas ● 2 oz/50 g toasted almonds ● shredded/desiccated coconut ● 2 or 3 types of chutney ● poppadoms or deep-fried prawn crackers.

From the store cupboard ● butter – Worcestershire sauce – Tabasco sauce – garlic – chilli peppers – salt – pepper – curry powder.

Work schedule ● Make the Cream caramel. Start cooking the Chicken Calcutta. Begin the pilaf rice (see p. 29). Prepare the Savoury tuna toasts.

Savoury tuna toasts

4 thick slices bread, toasted
¾ lb/350 g canned tuna
4/3 tbsp mayonnaise
4 drops lemon juice
4 drops Worcestershire sauce
4 drops Tabasco sauce
1 lettuce heart, finely shredded
1 tbsp capers
1 tomato, quartered
1 hard-boiled egg, quartered

Flake the tuna and mix with all the other ingredients except for the tomato and hard-boiled egg; heap the mixture on to the slices of toast and garnish with tomato wedges and the quarters of hard-boiled egg.

Preparation: 15 minutes.

Chicken Calcutta
(pressure cooker method)

1 medium-sized onion, sliced
1 clove garlic
½ chilli pepper
2 ripe tomatoes or 1 tbsp tomato paste
1 small piece fresh ginger root, finely chopped
(or ½ tsp ground ginger)
¼ cup/2 oz/50 g butter

⅔ cup/5 fl oz/150 ml natural yogurt
1 2¾-lb/1.2-kg chicken, cut into 8 portions
1½-2 tbsp curry powder
salt
½ cup/4 fl oz/125 ml light/single cream
4 portions pilaf rice (see p. 29)
a selection of the following side dishes:
sliced banana, seedless white raisins/sultanas, toasted almonds, shredded/desiccated coconut, 2 or 3 types of chutney, fried poppadoms, deep-fried prawn crackers.

Deep fry the onion in plenty of very hot oil until golden brown and crisp. Grind/mince the fried onion, garlic, chilli pepper, tomatoes or tomato paste and ginger. Melt the butter in a pressure cooker, add the yogurt and the ground/minced onion mixture and boil for 4 minutes. Place the chicken pieces in the pressure cooker and add the curry powder, salt and cream. Close the pressure cooker, bring up to pressure and cook for 10 minutes. Reduce pressure, remove the chicken pieces and arrange in a heated serving dish with the curry sauce. Serve the pilaf rice separately and place small bowls of sambals within reach of each guest.

Preparation: 20 minutes.
Total time: 50 minutes.

MENU 50

Hawaiian chicken salad
Scampi flamed in whisky
Boiled rice
Poires belle Hélène

Shopping list

¾ lb/350 g cooked chicken or turkey breast ● 1 fresh pineapple ● 1 small jar mayonnaise ● curry powder ● 1 lettuce ● 1¼ lb/600 g raw shelled frozen scampi ● 11 oz/300 g risotto rice ● 1 can pears ● 2 portions vanilla ice cream ● 4 oz/125 g plain chocolate ● 2 oz/50 g candied/crystallised violets.

From the store cupboard ● lemon – Tabasco sauce – Worcestershire sauce – wine vinegar – salt – sunflower oil – cocktail cherries – milk – butter – clarified butter (see p. 11) – whisky.

Work schedule ● Chill the pears in the refrigerator. Prepare the chicken salad. Cook the rice. Make the chocolate sauce (see p.129) and keep hot. Cook the scampi.

Hawaiian chicken salad

2 tbsp wine vinegar
1 tbsp mild curry powder
2 tbsp wine vinegar
6/4 tbsp mayonnaise
4 drops Tabasco sauce
4 drops Worcestershire sauce
juice of ½ lemon
¾ lb/350 g cooked chicken or turkey breast,
cut into thin strips
3 slices fresh pineapple, cut into strips
4 lettuce leaves
4 cocktail cherries

Heat the oil in a small saucepan, add the curry powder and cook over a moderate heat for 2 minutes; pour in the vinegar, continue cooking until the vinegar has reduced to half its original volume and leave to cool. Blend the curry, vinegar and oil mixture with the mayonnaise, Tabasco and Worcestershire sauce and lemon juice. Pour on to the chicken and pineapple and mix well. Place portions of the salad on lettuce leaves on individual plates. Garnish with a few small pieces of pineapple and cocktail cherries.

Preparation: 10 minutes.
Total time: 30 minutes.

Scampi flamed in whisky
(can be cooked at the table)

1¼ lb/600 g raw shelled frozen scampi
4/3 tbsp clarified butter
salt
5/3 tbsp whisky
4 portions plain boiled rice

Heat the clarified butter in a frying pan. When the butter is very hot, add the scampi. Sauté briefly and sprinkle lightly with salt. Pour in the whisky and heat; set alight and flame the scampi. Serve with very hot plain boiled rice.

Preparation: 8 minutes.

Poires belle Hélène

2 portions vanilla ice cream
1 can pears
2 oz/50 g candied/crystallized violets
hot chocolate sauce (see p.129)

Place a scoop of ice cream in the bottom of individual glass dishes; top with one or two pear halves and decorate with the candied/crystallized violets. Serve the hot chocolate sauce separately in a sauceboat or jug.

Preparation: 10 minutes.

MENU 51

Stuffed eggs
Lamb chops/cutlets with cream and brandy
Minted peas
Banana mousse

Shopping list

¼ lb/125 g canned cooked shrimp/prawns ● 2¼ lb/1 kg lamb chops/cutlets ● 1 large carton heavy/double cream ● 4 eggs ● ¾ lb/350 g Russian salad ● 1 packet frozen peas ● 1 lemon ● 1 tomato ● fresh sage leaves ● mint ● small bunch parsley ● 4 stuffed olives ● ½ oz/15 g powdered gelatine ● 4 bananas (3 very ripe) ● 7 oz/200 g vanilla ice cream.

From the store cupboard ● butter – paprika – brandy – Worcestershire sauce – mustard powder – cayenne pepper – clarified butter (see p. 11) – stock – flour – rum – sugar – salt – pepper.

Work schedule ● Hard-boil the eggs and cool in cold water. Make the Banana mousse and refrigerate. Stuff the eggs. Start cooking the lamb chops. Cook the peas with mint.

Stuffed eggs

4 hard-boiled eggs, peeled
4½ tbsp/generous 2 oz/60 g softened butter
1 tbsp paprika
1 tbsp brandy

20 drops Worcestershire sauce
1/2 tsp mustard powder
pinch cayenne pepper
salt
1/4 lb/125 g canned cooked shrimp/prawns
4 stuffed olives
3/4 lb/350 g Russian salad
small bunch parsley
1 tomato, quartered

Cut the hard-boiled eggs in half lengthwise and place the yolks in a bowl with the softened butter, paprika, brandy, Worcestershire sauce, mustard powder, cayenne pepper and salt and work together with a fork until the mixture is smooth and well blended. Chop half the shrimp/prawns, mix into the egg yolk mixture and use to stuff the hollows of the eggs. Garnish with the remaining whole shrimp/prawns and the halved stuffed olives. Arrange a layer of Russian salad on a serving dish, place the stuffed eggs on top and garnish with sprigs of parsley and tomato wedges.

Preparation: 15 minutes.
Total time: 30 minutes.

Lamb chops/cutlets with cream and brandy

2¹/4 lb/1 kg lamb chops/cutlets
2 tbsp flour
2 tbsp clarified butter (see p. 11)
1 tbsp brandy
6/4 tbsp heavy/double cream
6/4 tbsp stock
2 fresh sage leaves
1/2 tbsp lemon juice
salt
pepper

Season the lamb chops/cutlets with salt and pepper, coat lightly with flour and fry in the clarified butter in a large frying pan. When they are well browned on both sides, add the brandy, cream, stock and sage leaves. Cover and simmer gently for 10 minutes. Remove the chops/cutlets, and place on a heated serving dish. Add the lemon juice to the pan and adjust the seasoning; reduce a little if the sauce needs thickening. Pour the sauce over the chops/cutlets and serve without delay.

Preparation: 20 minutes.

Minted peas

Cook the peas according to the manufacturer's instructions; drain before they are completely cooked and dress with plenty of butter. Remove the saucepan from the heat and place a large bunch of mint on top of the peas; cover and keep warm for 10 minutes. Reheat gently just before serving.

Preparation: 15 minutes.

Banana mousse

½ oz/15 g powdered gelatine
¼ cup/4 fl oz/60 ml sugar syrup (half sugar, half water, boiled together)
4 bananas (3 very ripe)
½ cup/4 fl oz/125 ml rum
2 tbsp lemon juice
1¼ cups/7 oz/200 g vanilla ice cream
4/3 tbsp heavy/double cream, whipped

Soften the gelatine in a little cold water and then dissolve in the hot, not boiling, sugar syrup and leave to stand. Peel the 3 ripe bananas and place in the liquidizer with the rum and lemon juice. When the mixture is smooth, add the ice cream, a scoop at a time, blending after each addition. Add the gelatine and the hot sugar syrup. Pour the mixture into individual glass dishes and refrigerate. Before serving, decorate with the remaining sliced banana and whipped cream.

Preparation: 15 minutes.
Refrigeration: 45 minutes.

MENU 52

Lobster soup
Asparagus with remoulade sauce
Veal medallions with orange sauce
Duchesse potatoes
Coffee gâteau

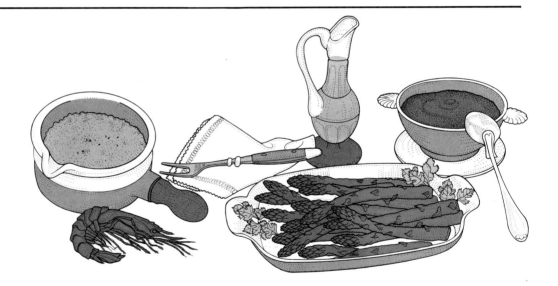

Shopping list

1¼ lb/600 g veal (upper leg or fillet), cut into 8 slices ● 1 can lobster soup (4 servings) ● 1 1¾-lb/800-g can white asparagus ● 1 small jar remoulade sauce (or see p. 74) ● 1 small carton light/single cream ● small bunch parsley ● 1 lemon ● 1 orange ● 1 lb/450 g floury potatoes ● 3 eggs ● 1 coffee gâteau.

From the store cupboard ● butter – sugar – wine vinegar – clarified butter (see p. 11) – milk – Grand Marnier – flour – stock – meat essence/extract – Marsala – salt – pepper – nutmeg.

Work schedule ● Start cooking the potatoes. Prepare and set out the ingredients for the Veal medallions. Put the Duchesse potatoes in the oven. Cook the veal and heat the Lobster soup.

Lobster soup

Prepare the soup according to the manufacturer's instructions. For a richer texture and taste, add a few tablespoons of light/single cream before serving, Do not allow the soup to boil once this has been added.

81

Asparagus with remoulade sauce

1 1¾-lb/800-g can white asparagus
1 lemon, cut into basket shape or lattice cut for
decorative effect
small bunch parsley
1 small jar remoulade sauce

Open the canned asparagus and drain well.
Arrange the asparagus on top of a clean white
serviette/napkin on a serving platter. Garnish
with the lemon and sprigs of parsley. Serve the
remoulade sauce separately.

Preparation: 5 minutes.

Veal medallions with orange sauce

peel of ¼ orange (no pith)
1¼ lb/600 g veal (upper leg or fillet), cut into 8
slices
salt
pepper
¼ cup/1 oz/25 g flour
3/2 tbsp clarified butter
1 tsp Grand Marnier
2 tbsp/1 oz/25 g butter (fresh, preferably un-
salted)
1 tbsp sugar
1 tbsp wine vinegar
2 tbsp Marsala
juice of ½ orange
6/4 tbsp light stock with added meat essence/
extract

Cut the orange peel into very fine strips and boil
in 2¼ cups/18 fl oz/500 ml lightly salted water for
5 minutes; refresh immediately in cold water.
Drain and set aside. Season the veal medallions
with salt and pepper, coat lightly with flour and
brown in hot clarified butter. Drain the veal and
sprinkle with the Grand Marnier; cover and
keep warm. Add the fresh butter and sugar to
the frying pan and caramelize; add the vinegar
and cook until it has evaporated. Pour in the
Marsala and orange juice and boil until the
sauce is reduced to half its original volume. Add
the stock and the orange peel, stir and return the
veal to the frying pan for 30 seconds to absorb
the flavour. Serve without delay.

Preparation: 20 minutes.

Duchesse potatoes

1 lb/450 g floury potatoes

1 cup/8 fl oz/225 ml milk
2½ tbsp/generous 1 oz/30 g butter
salt
pepper
pinch nutmeg
2 egg yolks and a little egg white
1 beaten egg for glazing

Peel the potatoes and boil in a mixture of water
and milk. Drain well and mash while still boiling
hot. Transfer the mashed potatoes to a heavy
saucepan and cook over a low heat to dry,
stirring and turning with a wooden spoon.
Remove from the heat, add the butter in small
pieces, together with the salt, pepper and
nutmeg. Beat in the egg yolks one at a time,
then the egg white. Work the mixture until it is
smooth and compact. Fill an icing bag with the
mixture and pipe into mounds on a buttered
baking sheet. Brush lightly with beaten egg and
brown in a preheated oven at 375°F/190°C/mk 5
for about 20 minutes.

Preparation: 15 minutes.
Total time: 45 minutes.

MENU 53

Quiche Lorraine
Liver with bacon and olives
French bean salad
Mangoes flamed in liqueur

Shopping list

1 lb/450 g liver, thinly sliced ● 5 oz/150 g frozen shortcrust pastry ● 1 packet frozen French beans ● 6 thin slices smoked streaky bacon ● 5 oz/150 g salt bacon/belly of pork ● 3 eggs ● 12 green olives ● ½ pint/300 ml light/single cream ● 1 small carton natural yogurt ● 2 fresh sage leaves ● small bunch parsley ● 4 fresh or canned mangoes ● 2 oranges ● 1 lemon.

From the store cupboard ● butter – flour – dry white wine – paprika – Grand Marnier – banana cream liqueur or maraschino – sugar – olive oil – vinegar – salt – pepper – brandy.

Work schedule ● Make the quiche and put in the oven. Cook and dress the beans. Prepare the ingredients for the mango dessert. Cook the liver.

Quiche Lorraine

5 oz/150 g frozen shortcrust pastry
6 thin slices smoked streaky bacon
1¾ cups/½ pint/300 ml light/single cream
3 eggs
pinch salt
2½ tbsp/generous 1 oz/30 g butter

Line a well-buttered quiche dish 8 in/20 cm in diameter with the shortcrust pastry and prick with a fork. Blanch the bacon in boiling water for 30 seconds and refresh immediately in cold water. Drain and pat dry. Place the bacon in a frying pan and sauté gently until the fat becomes transparent. Chop the bacon into small pieces and scatter over the bottom of the pastry-lined quiche dish. Lightly beat the cream, eggs and a pinch of salt and pour over the bacon. Dot the surface with flakes of butter. Cook in a pre-heated oven at 350°F/180°C/mk 4 for 20 minutes; lower the oven temperature and cook for a further 10 minutes. Remove from the oven and leave for 5 minutes before serving.

Preparation: 45 minutes.

Liver with bacon and olives

generous ½ cup/5 oz/150 g salt bacon/belly of pork, coarsely chopped
3 tbsp/1½ oz/40 g butter
1 lb/450 g liver, thinly sliced
1 tbsp flour
1 tsp paprika
5/3 tbsp dry white wine
2 fresh sage leaves
12 pitted green olives
1 small carton natural yogurt
salt
pepper

Sauté the bacon/belly of pork lightly in the butter. Coat the slices of liver with flour and add to the bacon and butter. As soon as the liver

changes colour add the paprika, wine, sage and olives. Stir briefly before adding the yogurt, parsley, salt and pepper. Serve at once.

Preparation: 15 minutes.

Mangoes flamed in liqueur
(can be prepared at the table)

4 ripe mangoes
2½ tbsp/generous 1 oz/30 g butter
4/3 tbsp sugar
4/3 tbsp orange juice
1 tbsp lemon juice

2 tbsp Grand Marnier
2 tbsp banana cream liqueur or maraschino
4/3 tbsp brandy

Peel the mangoes, cut in half and remove the stone. Fry the mangoes in the butter, turning them carefully two or three times; sprinkle in the sugar, orange juice, lemon juice, Grand Marnier and the banana cream liqueur or maraschino. Boil for a minute or two, turning the mangoes, add the brandy and flame.

Preparation: 8 minutes.

MENU 54

Valtellina bresaola (dried salt beef)
Country style risotto
Turkey breasts with cheese and ham
Mixed salad
Assorted cheeses

Shopping list

1¼ lb/600 g turkey breasts, boned ● 7 oz/200 g Valtellina bresaola (dried salt beef) ● 4 thin slices prosciutto/raw ham ● 4 thin slices of Gruyère, Emmental or Fontina cheese (or 4 processed cheese slices) ● 3 fresh sausages (preferably Italian fresh pork sausages) ● 1 egg ● 1 8-oz/225-g packet of frozen mixed vegetables ● 14 oz/400 g risotto rice ● mixed salad ingredients ● assorted cheeses.

From the store cupboard ● butter – stock – onion – dry white wine – freshly grated Parmesan cheese – breadcrumbs – olive oil – wine vinegar – salt – pepper.

Work schedule ● Trim, wash and dry the salad. Start cooking the risotto; once half the stock has been added, prepare the turkey breasts.

Country style risotto

2 cups/14 oz/400 g risotto rice
8 oz/225 g frozen mixed vegetables
4¼ cups/1¾ pints/1 liter stock, preferably home-made
6 tbsp/3 oz/80 g butter
1 tbsp finely chopped onion
3 fresh sausages (preferably Italian pork sausages)
2/3 cup/5 fl oz/150 ml dry white wine
4/3 tbsp freshly grated Parmesan cheese

Skin the sausages, break up the sausage meat and fry with the chopped onion in one-third of the butter. Add the rice and stir briefly; pour in the wine and continue cooking until the wine has evaporated. Add half the boiling stock together with the frozen vegetables. Cook the risotto for 18-20 minutes, stirring from time to time and adding more stock (¼-½ cup at a time) when the risotto begins to dry out. When the rice is tender

but still firm and moist, remove from the heat and dot the surface with the remaining butter cut into small pieces; sprinkle with the grated Parmesan cheese and mix with a wooden spoon.

Preparation: 35 minutes.

Turkey breasts with cheese and ham

1¼ lb/600 g boned turkey breasts, cut into 4 slices and beaten to even thickness
1 beaten egg

3/2 tbsp breadcrumbs
1/4 cup/2 oz/50 g butter
salt
4 thin slices of prosciutto/raw ham
4 slices Gruyère, Emmental or Fontina cheese
(or 4 processed cheese slices)

Dip the turkey slices in the beaten egg and coat with breadcrumbs; sauté in butter. Place on a baking sheet, sprinkle with salt and cover with a slice of ham and cheese. Broil/grill very briefly to melt the cheese and serve at once while the cheese is still hot.

Preparation: 15 minutes.

MENU 55

Mulligatawny soup
Chicken à la king
Pilaf rice
Singapore sundae

Shopping list

1¼ lb/600 g chicken breasts ● 1 can Mulligatawny soup (4 servings) ● 1 7-oz/200-g can cooked sweet peppers ● 1 can pineapple rings ● 1 carton light/single cream ● 1 carton heavy/double cream ● 11 oz/300 g long grain rice ● 2 eggs ● 5 oz/150 g button mushrooms ● 1 carrot ● 1 stick celery ● 11 oz/300 g vanilla ice cream.

From the store cupboard ● butter – white wine – bay leaf – onion – stock – glacé cherries – sherry – kirsch – salt – paprika.

Work schedule ● Boil the chicken breasts in a pressure cooker. Place the sundae dishes in the refrigerator to chill. Start the pilaf rice (see p. 29). Whip the cream for the Singapore sundae. Prepare the Chicken à la king and heat the Mulligatawny soup. Finish the Singapore sundaes.

Chicken à la king

1¼ cups/5 oz/150 g button mushrooms
2½ tbsp/generous 1 oz/30 g butter
1 tbsp paprika
1 7-oz/200-g can cooked sweet peppers, cut into thin strips
⅔ cup/5 fl oz/150 ml light/single cream
salt
1¼ lb/600 g boned chicken breasts, boiled for 8 minutes in a pressure cooker with:
    ½ cup/4 fl oz/125 ml white wine
    ½ cup/4 fl oz/125 ml water
    ½ carrot, 1 small stick celery, ½ bay leaf, salt
2 tbsp sherry
2 egg yolks

Wipe the mushrooms with a damp cloth and slice; sauté briefly in the butter. Stir in the paprika followed by the sweet peppers, three-quarters of the cream and the salt. Cover and cook until the mushrooms are almost tender. Drain and dice the chicken breasts or cut into thin strips across the grain of the flesh and add to the ingredients in the pan. Cook for a few minutes. Add the sherry, bring back to the boil and then lower the heat. Stir in the egg yolks, beaten with a fork into the remaining cream, and simmer over a very low heat, stirring constantly, to thicken. Do not allow to boil. Transfer to a heated serving dish. Serve the pilaf rice separately.

Preparation: 35 minutes.

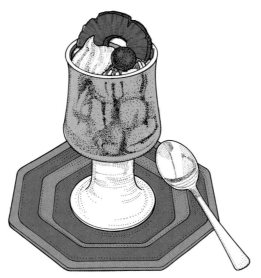

Singapore sundae

2 cups/11 oz/300 g vanilla ice cream
4 pineapple rings
2 tbsp kirsch
6/4 tbsp sweetened whipped cream
4 glacé cherries

Place a scoop of vanilla ice cream in each chilled sundae dish and top with a pineapple ring: sprinkle with a little kirsch and decorate with whipped cream and a glacé cherry.

Preparation: 10 minutes.

MENU 56

Game pâté with hot toast
Quick veal in cream and wine sauce
Creamed potatoes
Coffee log

Shopping list

1¼ lb/600 g thinly sliced veal (upper leg or fillet) • 1 can coarse game pâté • 1 white loaf of bread • 1 small carton light/single cream • 1 can or packet instant creamed potatoes • 1 lemon • small bunch parsley • 1 coffee log.

From the store cupboard • flour – clarified butter (see p. 11) – dry white wine – milk – butter – brandy – onion – salt – pepper.

Work schedule • Prepare the veal in cream and wine sauce. Make the creamed potatoes. Prepare the toast.

Quick veal in cream and wine sauce

1¼ lb/600 g thinly sliced veal (upper leg or fillet)
2 tbsp flour
3/2 tbsp clarified butter
1 tbsp finely chopped onion
¼ cup/2½ fl oz/75 ml dry white wine
⅔ cup/5 fl oz/150 ml light/single cream
salt
pepper
1 tbsp brandy
1 tbsp lemon juice
1 tbsp chopped parsley

Cut the veal slices into 1-in/2.5-cm squares. Place the veal and flour in a bowl and mix with the fingers to coat the pieces lightly with flour. Heat the clarified butter in a wide frying pan until sizzling hot; add the veal and cook over a very high heat, stirring with a wooden spatula. Remove the veal with a slotted spoon, drain well

and keep warm between two hot plates. Fry the onion lightly in the same pan; pour in the wine and continue cooking until the liquid has partially evaporated. Add the cream and boil to reduce the sauce by half. Season with salt and pepper, add the brandy and lemon juice and bring back to the boil. Return the veal to the pan and stir briefly. Remove the pan from the heat; cover

and leave to stand for about 1 minute. Pipe the creamed potatoes around the edges of a large heated serving platter, leaving a well in the center, and pour the veal and sauce into the middle. Garnish with chopped parsley and serve without delay.

Preparation: 15 minutes.

MENU 57

Buttered ribbon noodles
Quail and sausage kebabs
Steamed buttered leeks
Lychees with maraschino

Shopping list

6 quails • 12 small spicy sausages • 14 oz/400 g fresh or 11 oz/ 300 g dried egg noodles (fettuccine) • 1 small carton light/ single cream • 4 oz/125 g freshly grated Parmesan cheese • 1 1¾-lb/800-g can lychees • ½ wholemeal loaf of bread • 2¼ lb/1 kg leeks • bay leaves • fresh sage • 5 oz/150 g vanilla ice cream.

From the store cupboard • butter – breadcrumbs (toasted or fresh) – clarified butter (see p. 11) – maraschino – salt – pepper.

Work schedule • Soak the leeks. Spoon the lychees into individual sundae dishes and refrigerate. Prepare the kebabs. Drain and steam the leeks. Set plenty of salted water to boil for the noodles. Make the sauce for the lychees. Start broiling/grilling the kebabs. Put the leeks in the oven. Cook the noodles.

Buttered ribbon noodles

14 oz/400 g fresh or 11 oz/300 g dried egg noodles
½ cup/4 oz/125 g butter
10/6 tbsp light/single cream
6/4 tbsp freshly grated Parmesan cheese
salt
freshly ground pepper

Cook the ribbon noodles for 7 minutes in plenty

of boiling salted water until just tender. Melt a quarter of the butter in a large frying pan; drain the noodles (reserving 3/2 tbsp of the water) and add to the butter in the pan. Moisten with the cooking water and stir over a low heat. Add small quantities at a time of cream, butter and grated Parmesan cheese, alternating them in this order; gently stir and turn the noodles, using two forks, until thoroughly coated with the sauce. Add freshly ground pepper and serve immediately.

Preparation: 10 minutes.

Quail and sausage kebabs

12 small spicy sausages
6 quails
6 fresh sage leaves
salt
pepper
thick slices wholemeal bread, dried and crisped in the oven
6 bay leaves
5/3 tablespoons clarified butter

Prick the sausages with a fork and heat in a large pan of simmering water for a few minutes. Cut each quail in half lengthwise, place ½ a sage leaf inside the cavity and season lightly with salt and

Opposite:
Menu 42, page 66

salt
pepper
¼ cup/2 oz/50 g butter
*2 tbsp finely ground toasted or fine fresh bread-
crumbs*

Cut off the root end of the leeks and the green part, retaining the white section. Make an incision about 1 in/2.5 cm deep into the top and place in a bowl of cold water to soak away any grit and earth. Steam the leeks over salted water for 10-15 minutes, depending on their thickness. When they are tender, place in a buttered ovenproof dish and sprinkle with salt, freshly ground pepper, melted butter and bread-crumbs. Bake in a preheated oven at 350°F/180°C/mk 4 for 10 minutes. Do not allow to brown. Arrange on a large heated serving platter with the quail and sausage kebabs.

Preparation: 15 minutes.
Total time: 1 hour.

Lychees with maraschino

1 1¾-lb/800-g can lychees
scant 1 cup/5 oz/150 g vanilla ice cream
6/4 tbsp maraschino

Cut the lychees in half and remove the stone. Drain off the liquid (reserve a quarter for later use) and chill the lychees for as long as possible. Place the vanilla ice cream in a bowl and gradually beat in the maraschino and the re-served lychee juice; place the lychees in indi-vidual bowls and pour over the maraschino-flavoured ice cream just before serving.

Preparation: 10 minutes.

pepper. Cut the bread the same size as the sausages and thread the ingredients on to skewers, alternating bread, sausage, ½ quail, ½ bay leaf; use several skewers. Make sure the cavity of each quail is firmly pressed against the sausage. Brush with clarified butter and broil/grill slowly or fry gently in a large frying pan. Turn the kebabs frequently and brush with more clarified butter when necessary.

Preparation: 15 minutes.
Total time: 30 minutes.

Steamed buttered leeks

2¼ lb/1 kg leeks

MENU 58

Tropicana melon cocktail
Cream of mushroom soup
Porgy/gilt head bream en
papillote
Steamed potatoes
Mixed salad
Fruit salad with Grand Marnier

Shopping list

1 3½-lb/1.5-kg porgy/gilt head bream (or sea bream) ● 1 large or two small melons ● 1 lemon ● small bunch mint ● small bunch parsley ● 2¼ lb/1 kg new potatoes ● 4 oranges ● mixed salad ingredients ● 1 small carton light/single cream ● 1 can cream of mushroom soup (4 servings) ● 1 can pineapple rings ● 1 can peaches ● 1 can cherries.

From the store cupboard ● 2 shallots – tomato ketchup – cocktail cherries – cayenne pepper – dry white wine – gin – whisky – Grand Marnier – sunflower oil – olive oil – wine vinegar – salt – pepper – ground ginger.

Work schedule ● Prepare the melon cocktail and refrigerate. Peel the potatoes and start cooking in the steamer. Prepare the fish and place in the oven. Wash the salad and heat the mushroom soup. Make the fruit salad dessert and finish the melon cocktail.

Tropicana melon cocktail
(serve in glass sundae dishes)

1 large melon or two small melons
3/2 tbsp gin
3/2 tbsp whisky

Opposite:
Menu 51, page 79

1 tbsp ground ginger
1 tbsp lemon juice
3/2 tbsp tomato ketchup
generous pinch cayenne pepper
salt
4 cocktail cherries
4 fresh mint leaves

Use a melon baller to scoop out the flesh of the melon(s) and fill the sundae dishes two-thirds full with melon balls. Place the remaining melon flesh in the blender with the gin, whisky, ground ginger, lemon juice, tomato ketchup, cayenne pepper and a pinch of salt. Liquidize until the mixture is smooth, then pour over the melon balls and refrigerate for at least 45 minutes. Decorate with cocktail cherries and fresh mint leaves just before serving.

Preparation: 10 minutes.
Refrigeration: 45 minutes.

Cream of mushroom soup

Heat the soup according to the manufacturer's instructions. Shortly before serving, add a few tbsp light/single cream to improve the flavour and consistency. Do not allow to boil once the cream has been added.

Porgy/gilt head bream en papillote

1 3½-lb/1.5-kg porgy/gilt head bream (or sea bream)
2 cups/16 fl oz/450 ml dry white wine
salt
pepper
sunflower oil
2 sprigs parsley
2 shallots

Gut the fish and rinse in white wine only; sprinkle liberally with salt, freshly ground pepper and oil and place a few sprigs of parsley, tied in a small bunch, inside the cavity. Sprinkle the fish with the finely chopped shallots and enclose with the remaining parsley sprig in a large oiled sheet of greaseproof paper or foil. Bake in a preheated oven at 350°F/180°C/mk 4 for 20-25 minutes. Open up the case in which the fish has been cooked at the table.

Preparation: 5 minutes.
Total time: 30 minutes.

Fruit salad with Grand Marnier

4 canned pineapple rings
4 oranges, peel and pith removed
4 canned peach halves
4 canned cherries
3/2 tbsp Grand Marnier

Take 4 small dessert plates and on each arrange a pineapple ring with a whole orange in the center. Place a peach half, rounded side uppermost, on top of the orange and secure with a wooden cocktail stick. Place a cherry on the end of each cocktail stick and sprinkle each dessert with Grand Marnier.

Preparation: 10 minutes.

MENU 59

Mushroom pizza
Pork steaks with mustard
Salad with blue cheese dressing
Assorted cheeses

Shopping list

1¼ lb/600 g fillet or tenderloin of pork, cut into 8 steaks ● 1 ready-made pizza with extra ¼ lb/125 g button mushrooms for the topping ● assorted cheeses, including Roquefort or Gorgonzola ● 1 small carton light/single cream ● small bunch parsley ● mixed salad ingredients.

From the store cupboard ● butter – clarified butter (see p. 11) – white wine vinegar – Grand Marnier – oil – paprika – Dijon mustard – salt – pepper.

Work schedule ● Trim, wash and dry the salad. Prepare the pork steaks. Place the extra mushrooms on the pizza and preheat the oven. Make the Blue cheese dressing.

Pork steaks with mustard

1¼ lb/600 g fillet or tenderloin of pork, cut into 8 steaks
salt
pepper
2 level tbsp Dijon mustard
2 tbsp clarified butter
2 tbsp white wine vinegar
1 tbsp chopped parsley

Pound the pork steaks with a meat bat. Season with salt and pepper and coat each one completely with the Dijon mustard. Heat the clarified butter until very hot, and brown the steaks on both sides over high heat. Add the vinegar and the chopped parsley, lower the heat and continue cooking with the pan tightly covered until the pork is tender.

Preparation: 15 minutes.

Blue cheese dressing

1 tbsp wine vinegar

3/2 tbsp oil
2 tbsp/generous 1 oz/30 g Roquefort or Gorgon-
zola cheese
1 tbsp light/single cream
pinch paprika

Place the vinegar and oil in a small bowl and use a fork to crumble the cheese into it. Add the cream and paprika, mix well and pour over the salad just before serving.

MENU 60

Assorted cold meats
Consommé with sherry
Chicken paprika Hungarian style
Creamed potatoes
Hawaiian gâteau

Shopping list

7 oz/200 g assorted cold meats ● 1 can consommé (4 servings) ● 1 2¾-lb/1.2-kg oven-ready chicken ● 3½ oz/100 g fresh pork fat or salt bacon/belly of pork ● 1 small carton sour or heavy/double cream ● 1 small can tomato paste ● 1 can pineapple rings ● 1 can or packet instant creamed potatoes ● small bunch parsley ● 2 bananas ● 18 fl oz/500 ml milk ● 1 7-oz/200-g round sponge cake ● 1 small carton whipping cream.

From the store cupboard ● sherry (if possible use medium dry sherry in which 2 or 3 chilli peppers have been steeped for at least 2 days) – onion – paprika – dry white wine – stock – cloves – garlic – nutmeg – flour – bay leaf – thyme – pine nuts or almonds – sugar – kirsch – butter – salt – pepper.

Work schedule ● Set the Chicken paprika to cook in the pressure cooker. Make the creamed potatoes. Prepare the dessert.

Consommé with sherry

Serve the consommé in individual consommé bowls. Pass round a jug or small carafe of sherry in which the chilli peppers have marinated, so that each guest can adjust the flavouring as desired.

Chicken paprika Hungarian style
(pressure cooker method)

1 2¾-lb/1.2-kg oven-ready chicken, cut into 8 pieces
salt
pepper
nutmeg
flour
scant ½ cup/3½ oz/100 g fresh pork fat or salt bacon/belly of pork, finely diced
1 tbsp finely chopped onion
1 tbsp paprika
1 cup/8 fl oz/225 ml dry white wine
½ cup/4 fl oz/125 ml stock
½ cup/3 fl oz/90 ml sour or heavy/double cream
2 cloves
1 bouquet garni (bay leaf, thyme and parsley, tied together in a piece of muslin)
1 clove garlic
½ tbsp tomato paste

Season the chicken pieces with salt, pepper and a little grated nutmeg and coat lightly with flour. Melt the pork fat in the pressure cooker; turn up the heat a little and brown the chicken pieces; add the chopped onion and sauté lightly. Sprinkle with the paprika and stir in ½ tbsp

flour; continue cooking for a minute or two before adding the wine. When the wine has evaporated, pour in the stock and cream and add the cloves, bouquet garni, garlic and tomato paste. Stir well, place the lid on the pressure cooker, bring up to pressure and cook for 5 minutes. Reduce pressure and remove the chicken pieces; place on a bed of creamed potatoes in a deep preheated serving dish. Strain the juices from the pressure cooker and pour over the chicken.

Preparation: 20 minutes.
Total time: 25-30 minutes.

Hawaiian gâteau

1 7-oz/200-g round sponge cake
2 bananas
6/4 tbsp sweetened whipped cream
4 canned pineapple rings
6/4 tbsp sugar syrup (a mixture of half sugar, half water, boiled together until the sugar has totally dissolved)
1 tbsp kirsch
pine nuts or flaked almonds for garnish

Cut the sponge cake into two layers. Peel the bananas and slice thinly on to one of the layers. Spread with sweetened whipped cream and cover with the second layer of sponge. Arrange the pineapple rings on top and spoon over the sugar syrup mixed with the kirsch. Sprinkle with pine nuts or flaked almonds before serving.

Preparation: 10 minutes.

MENU 61

Neapolitan pizza
Peppered entrecôte steaks
Salad with tomato vinaigrette
Gorgonzola cheese with honey

Shopping list

4 9-oz/250-g boneless loin/entrecôte steaks ● 1 frozen Neapolitan pizza ● 1 small can green peppercorns ● 1 small carton light/single cream ● 1 small jar clear honey ● 10½ oz/ 300 g full-fat Gorgonzola cheese ● mixed green salad.

From the store cupboard ● clarified butter (see p. 11) – whisky or brandy – Dijon mustard – paprika – tomato ketchup – mustard powder – oil – wine vinegar – salt.

Work schedule ● Heat the pizza according to the manufacturer's instructions. Prepare the salad.

Mix the tomato vinaigrette. Prepare the Peppered entrecôte steaks.

Peppered entrecôte steaks
(can be cooked at the table)

4 9-oz/250-g boneless loin/entrecôte steaks
salt
2 tbsp clarified butter
3/2 tbsp whisky or brandy
3/2 tbsp green peppercorns, coarsely crushed
1 tbsp Dijon mustard
¹/₃ cup/2¹/₂ fl oz/70 ml light/single cream

Sprinkle the beef steaks lightly with salt and brown on both sides in very hot clarified butter; lower the heat and cook the steaks according to preference. Remove the steaks from the pan and set aside to keep warm between two hot plates. Add the whisky or brandy, peppercorns and the mustard (blended with the cream) to the juices and fat in the pan. Boil for 30 seconds and pour over the steaks.

Preparation: 10 minutes.

Tomato vinaigrette

1 tbsp paprika
¹/₂ tsp mustard powder
1 tbsp tomato ketchup
1 tbsp wine vinegar

3/2 tbsp olive oil
salt

Mix the paprika, mustard and tomato ketchup with the vinegar, then gradually beat in the oil with a fork or small whisk; add salt to taste. Pour over the salad just before serving.

Gorgonzola cheese with honey

Serve Gorgonzola cheese and hand round separately a small jug of clear honey as a sauce for the cheese.

MENU 62

Artichokes vinaigrette
Ribbon noodles with ham and mushrooms
Fillets of John Dory with capers
Steamed potatoes
Black Forest gâteau

Shopping list

4 fillets John Dory, turbot or brill ● 1 lb/450g fresh or 14 oz/400 g dry ribbon noodles (fettucine) ● 4 large globe artichokes ● fresh basil leaves ● 2 lemons ● small bunch parsley ● 2¼ lb/1 kg new potatoes ● 4 oz/125 g button mushrooms ● 3½ oz/100 g prosciutto/raw ham, machine sliced ● 3½ oz/100 g freshly grated Parmesan cheese ● 1 small bottle vinaigrette (or see p. 34) ● 2 oz/50 g capers ● 1 frozen Black Forest gâteau.

From the store cupboard ● butter – flour – salt – pepper.

Work schedule ● Boil the artichokes. Make the vinaigrette dressing (see p. 34). Set the water to boil for the noodles. Start cooking the fish and plunge the noodles into the boiling, salted water.

Artichokes vinaigrette

4 large artichokes
lemon juice

salt
small knob butter
1 cup/8 fl oz/225 ml vinaigrette dressing (see p. 34)

Wash and trim the artichokes and remove the outer older and tougher leaves. Trim the points of the leaves and rub all the cut surfaces immediately with lemon juice to prevent discolouration. Cut the stalk off very close to the artichoke base; as each artichoke is prepared, place into a large bowl of acidulated water (fresh lemon juice mixed with cold water). Place the artichokes upright in a large saucepan, add salt, a small knob of butter and enough cold water to just cover them. Boil the artichokes for 30-45 minutes or until they are tender. Drain and squeeze the artichokes gently just before serving to get rid of excess water. Place on a serving dish and hand round small bowls of vinaigrette.

Preparation: 55 minutes.

Fillets of John Dory with capers

4 fillets John Dory, turbot or brill, soaked in
lightly salted milk, drained and patted dry
flour
¼ cup + 1½ tbsp/2¾ oz/75 g butter
salt
pepper
2 tbsp capers, coarsely chopped
½-1 lemon, peel and pith removed
1 tbsp chopped parsley

Coat the fish fillets lightly in flour and fry for 5 minutes on each side in 2 tbsp/1 oz/25 g butter. Add a little salt and freshly ground pepper and transfer to a hot serving platter. Place the capers in a saucepan with the remaining butter and heat very gently until the butter has melted; the capers should warm through but should not fry. Add small segments of lemon; just before the capers and lemon show signs of coming to the boil, draw aside from the heat and pour over the fish fillets. Sprinkle with chopped parsley and serve without delay.

Preparation: 15 minutes.

Ribbon noodles with ham and mushrooms

1 lb/450 g fresh or 14 oz/400 g dry ribbon noodles
(fettucine)
4 oz/125 g button mushrooms
¼ cup + 1½ tbsp/2¾ oz/75 g butter
1 tsp finely chopped fresh basil (or pinch dried
basil)
scant ½ cup/3½ oz/100 g prosciutto/raw ham,
machine sliced
salt
pepper

Bring a large saucepan of salted water to the boil and add the noodles; meanwhile, slice the mushrooms and sauté gently in half the butter for 4 minutes; add the chopped basil and the prosciutto/raw ham cut into strips and season with salt and freshly ground pepper. Cover and leave over the lowest heat possible for a minute or two. When the noodles are tender but still firm, drain and place in a deep heated serving dish, dot with the remaining butter cut into small pieces and add half the grated Parmesan cheese. Mix gently but thoroughly. Pour the mushrooms and cooking juices over the noodles and serve at once. Serve the remaining grated Parmesan cheese separately.

Preparation: 15 minutes.

Savoury pancakes
Pigeons en cocotte
Steamed potatoes
Viennese sundae

Shopping list

1¼ lb/600 g mushrooms, preferably *cèpes* or *porcini* ● 4 pigeons ● 1 fairly thick slice salt bacon/belly of pork ● 3 oz/80 g canned mushrooms caps ● 2 eggs ● 2¼ lb/1 kg new potatoes ● 12 shallots ● small bunch parsley ● thyme ● 1 small carton heavy/double cream ● 11 oz/300 g vanilla ice cream ● 1 tbsp instant coffee ● 2 oz/50 g finger biscuits (langues de chat).

From the store cupboard ● butter – flour – milk – vanilla flavoured superfine/caster sugar – oil – onion – garlic – white wine – meat essence/ extract – bay leaf – coffee – salt – pepper.

Work schedule ● Prepare the pancake batter (see p. 30) and make the coffee to pour over the Viennese sundae. Start cooking the pigeons. Make the pancakes. Prepare the mushroom filling for the pancakes. Set the potatoes in the steamer to cook (see p. 40). Fill the pancakes with the mushroom mixture. Whip the cream.

Savoury pancakes

1¼ lb/600 g mushrooms, preferably cèpes *or* porcini
1 tbsp chopped onion
3 tbsp/1½ oz/40 g butter
1 clove of garlic, crushed
1 tbsp chopped parsley
¼ cup/2 fl oz/60 ml white wine
salt
pepper
8 pancakes (see p. 30)

Clean the mushrooms and slice thinly. Sauté the onion gently in the butter until pale golden brown. Add the crushed garlic, the chopped parsley and the mushrooms and cook over a very high heat for 5 minutes; pour in the wine and cook for a further 6 minutes over a fairly high heat. Season with salt and pepper at the last minute. Divide the mushrooms between the pancakes and fold each one into quarters. Transfer the pancakes, overlapping slightly if necessary, to a buttered ovenproof dish and place in a hot oven for 5 minutes.

Preparation (with ready-made pancakes): 15 minutes, otherwise 35 minutes.
Total time: 50 minutes.

Pigeons en cocotte

4 pigeons
salt
pepper
¼ cup + 1 tbsp/2½ oz/70 g butter
1 fairly thick slice salted bacon/belly of pork
12 shallots, peeled and trimmed
6/4 tbsp dry white wine
½ tsp meat essence/extract
bouquet garni comprising:
    ½ bay leaf
    4 sprigs parsley, with stalks
    1 sprig thyme, enclosed in muslin
⅔ cup/3 oz/80 g canned mushroom caps

Wash and dry the pigeons and season with salt and pepper. Brown gently in the butter. Once the birds are evenly browned, remove from the pan, drain and wrap in foil so that they remain moist. Cut the salt bacon/belly of pork into small strips and add with the shallots to the juices and butter in the pan; cook until lightly browned.

Remove the bacon with a slotted spoon and set aside. Drain off the excess fat, add the wine to the juices and allow to reduce slightly. Pour in the meat essence/extract dissolved in a little hot water and reduce the liquid to one third of its original volume. Return the pigeons, onions and salt bacon/belly of pork to the pan; add the bouquet garni, cover tightly and cook in a preheated oven at 350°F/180°C/mk 4 for 30 minutes. Shortly before serving, add the mushrooms, allowing them just enough time to warm through.

Preparation: 15 minutes.
Total time: 45 minutes.

Viennese sundae

6/4 tbsp heavy/double cream
3/2 tsp vanilla flavoured superfine/caster sugar
1 tbsp powdered instant coffee
scant 2 cups/11 oz/300 g vanilla ice cream
½ cup/4 fl oz/125 ml very strong black coffee, unsweetened and chilled
2 oz/50 g finger biscuits (langues de chat)

Whip the cream until firm and fold in the vanilla flavoured sugar, together with the instant coffee

powder. Scoop the ice cream into sundae dishes and pour a little iced coffee over each portion; top with the sweetened whipped cream and decorate with finger biscuits as illustrated.

Preparation: 10 minutes.

MENU 64

Peking lobster
Cream of asparagus soup
Chicken breasts Caruso
Spring salad
Strawberries and cream

Shopping list

2 11-oz/300-g lobsters ● 1¼ lb/600 g chicken or turkey breasts ● 1 can asparagus soup (4 servings) ● 9 oz/250 g bean sprouts ● 1 small jar shrimp/prawn cocktail sauce (or see p. 26) ● 3½ oz/100 g prosciutto/raw ham, machine sliced (at least one slice per chicken breast) ● 1 packet processed cheese slices ● 1 egg ● 12 fl oz/350 ml heavy/double cream ● 1 small pineapple ● 1 lettuce ● mixed salad ingredients ● 1 lb/450 g fresh or frozen strawberries.

From the store cupboard ● butter – Tabasco sauce – cayenne pepper – Worcestershire sauce – 1 lemon – flour – sugar – vanilla flavoured superfine/caster sugar – kirsch – salt – pepper.

Work schedule ● Hard-boil the eggs. Prepare the chicken breasts for cooking; wash and drain the salad. Dress the lobsters. Cook the chicken breasts and heat the asparagus soup. Prepare the strawberry dessert.

1 packet processed cheese slices
3¹/₂ oz/100 g prosciutto/raw ham, machine sliced
2 tbsp flour
3 tbsp/1¹/₂ oz/40 g butter

Cut the chicken or turkey breasts into slices and pound lightly to an even thickness; season with salt and pepper and lay out flat. Place a processed cheese slice and a slice of prosciutto/raw ham on top and secure with a wooden cocktail stick. Coat lightly with flour and fry gently in butter until the meat is cooked through.

Preparation: 15 minutes.

Strawberries and cream

generous 1 cup/9 fl oz/250 ml heavy/double cream
1 tbsp vanilla flavoured superfine/caster sugar
1 lb/450 g fresh or frozen strawberries
3/2 tbsp sugar
2 tbsp kirsch

Whip the cream until firm, gradually adding the vanilla flavoured sugar. Wash and hull the strawberries and sprinkle with sugar and kirsch. Spoon into sundae dishes or large glass goblets and decorate with the sweetened whipped cream.

Preparation: 10 minutes.

Peking lobster

2 11-oz/300-g lobsters, boiled and cooled
9 oz/250 g bean sprouts
2 slices fresh pineapple, cut into small cubes
¹/₂ cup/4 fl oz/125 g shrimp/prawn cocktail sauce
8 drops Tabasco sauce
¹/₂ tsp Worcestershire sauce
pinch cayenne pepper
juice of ¹/₂ lemon
a few crisp lettuce leaves
1 hard-boiled egg, quartered or sliced

Split the lobsters in half lengthwise and rinse in cold water to wash away the soft creamy part. Remove the firm white flesh from the shell and cut into small cubes. Wash and dry the lobster shells. Place the bean sprouts in a sieve or colander, rinse under cold running water and chop coarsely. Place the bean sprouts in a bowl with the lobster flesh, pineapple and the cocktail sauce mixed with the Tabasco and Worcestershire sauce, cayenne pepper and lemon juice. Stir carefully so that the lobster is well coated with the dressing. Line the lobster shells with lettuce leaves, fill with the lobster, bean sprout and pineapple mixture and garnish with pieces of hard-boiled egg.

Preparation, including time allowed for boiling lobsters: 50 minutes.

Cream of asparagus soup

For a richer soup with a more subtle taste and creamier consistency, add 6/4 tbsp heavy/double cream as the soup is heating. Do not boil.

Chicken breasts Caruso

1¹/₄ lb/600 g chicken or turkey breasts
salt
pepper

Asparagus with mayonnaise
Boula-boula (Tahitian soup)
Fillets of sole Saint-Germain
Béarnaise sauce
Pommes de terre noisette
Peaches flamed in kirsch

Shopping list

1 lb/450 g sole fillets ● 1¾ lb/800 g canned large asparagus (white variety if possible) ● 1 9-oz/250-g jar mayonnaise ● 1 large can peaches (8 halves) ● 1 jar Béarnaise sauce ● 1 packet or can cream of pea soup (2 servings) ● 1 can turtle soup (2 servings) ● 1 small carton whipping cream ● small bunch parsley ● 1 tomato ● 2¼ lb/1 kg potatoes.

From the store cupboard ● butter – fresh breadcrumbs – kirsch – salt – pepper.

Work schedule ● Place the prepared potatoes in the oven (see p. 21). Drain the asparagus and arrange on a serving platter. Cook the fillets of sole; meanwhile, heat the soup. Just before sitting down to dinner, place the peaches over a low heat in their juice to warm through.

Asparagus with mayonnaise

1¾ lb/800 g canned large asparagus
1 9-oz/250-g jar mayonnaise
small bunch parsley
1 tomato, cut into wedges

Drain the asparagus well and place on a folded linen serviette on a serving platter, arranging the sprigs of parsley and the tomato on the part of the platter not covered by the cloth. Serve the mayonnaise separately.

Preparation: 5 minutes.

Boula-boula (Tahitian soup)

1 packet or can cream of pea soup (2 servings)
1 can turtle soup (2 servings)
4 tbsp whipped unsweetened cream

Make the pea soup according to the instructions on the packet or can; if possible, make the soup a little thicker than indicated. Heat the turtle soup without diluting it and stir into the hot pea soup; ladle the mixture into ovenproof dishes; float 1 tbsp whipped cream on the surface of each and place under a very hot broiler/grill for a few seconds.

Preparation: 10 minutes.

Fillets of sole Saint-Germain

1 lb/450 g sole fillets
3 tbsp/1½ oz/40 g butter
freshly toasted fine breadcrumbs
salt
pepper

Flatten the fillets of sole gently, brush with melted butter and coat with the breadcrumbs. Arrange in a single layer in a shallow ovenproof dish and broil/grill for 3 minutes; turn the fillets carefully and cook for a further 2 minutes. Serve with pommes de terre noisette and hand round Béarnaise sauce separately.

Preparation: 10 minutes.

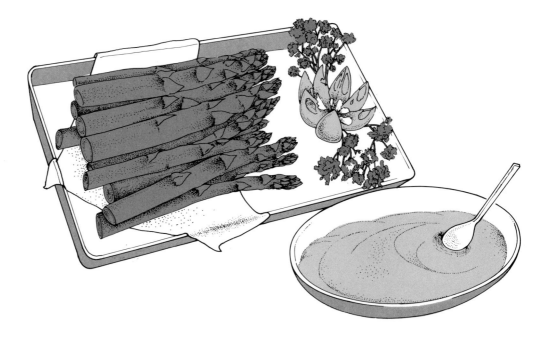

Peaches flamed in kirsch

8 canned peach halves
½ cup/4 fl oz/125 ml kirsch

Warm the peach halves gently in the juice from the can; remove the peaches from the juice or syrup with a slotted spoon and place on a very hot serving dish. Heat the kirsch in a small saucepan, set alight and pour over the peaches, shaking the dish gently so that they flame more freely (this can be done at the table if preferred).

Preparation: 10 minutes.

MENU 66

Chinese crispy fried noodles (Chow Mein)
Veal steaks with Armagnac
Duchesse potatoes
Fresh fruit salad in Champagne

Shopping list

8 2-oz/50-g veal steaks, cut from the upper leg ● 11 oz/300 g Chinese egg noodles ● 1 small carton light/single cream ● 6 eggs ● 1 2-oz/50-g slice cooked ham ● fresh fruit in season ● 1 2-oz/50-g can small shrimp/prawns ● 1 packet dried mushrooms (preferably Italian *porcini* or French *cèpes*) ● 5 canned Chinese mushrooms (if unavailable use cultivated mushrooms) ● 4 large cultivated mushrooms ● small bunch parsley ● 2¼ lb/1 kg potatoes ● ¼ bottle Champagne ● 1 scallion/spring onion or small leek ● 1 shallot ● 1 loaf of bread.

From the store cupboard ● butter – soy sauce – oil – meat essence/extract – Armagnac – 1 lemon – sugar – salt – pepper.

Work schedule ● Peel and dice the fruit; add the Champagne and chill. Set the potatoes to boil for the Duchesse potatoes (see p. 82). Set out the ingredients for the veal steaks. Place the Duchesse potatoes and the slices of bread in the oven. Cook the Chinese noodles. Sauté and flame the veal.

Chinese crispy fried noodles (Chow Mein)

11 oz/300 g Chinese egg noodles
5/3 tbsp oil
1 2-oz/50-g can small shrimp/prawns
1 2-oz/50-g slice cooked ham, finely diced
5 canned Chinese mushrooms (if unavailable use cultivated mushrooms)
2 eggs
1 tbsp soy sauce
1 tbsp chopped stem of scallion/spring onion or leek

Boil the noodles in plenty of salted water until tender; drain and refresh immediately in cold water to which 1 tbsp of oil has been added. Spread out on a damp cloth to dry off excess moisture. Heat the oil in a wok or large frying pan and sauté the drained shrimp/prawns, the diced ham and the coarsely chopped mushrooms for a minute or two. Add the noodles and stir-fry over high heat for 3-4 minutes. Break the eggs into a cup and stir to break up the yolks (do not beat); turn down the heat, pour in the eggs and continue frying for a further 3 minutes, stirring constantly. Sprinkle with soy sauce and chopped scallion/spring onion or leek. Serve without delay.

Preparation: 15 minutes.

Veal steaks with Armagnac

8 slices bread
2½ tbsp/1½ oz/40 g butter
8 dried mushrooms, soaked in lukewarm water for 15 minutes, drained and chopped
1 finely chopped shallot
8 2-oz/50-g veal steaks, cut from the upper leg
salt
pepper
4 tbsp Armagnac
½ tsp meat essence/extract dissolved in 2 tbsp hot water
6/4 tbsp light/single cream
1 tsp lemon juice
garnish: 4 button mushrooms, stalks removed chopped parsley

Cut a small hole in the top of each mushroom,

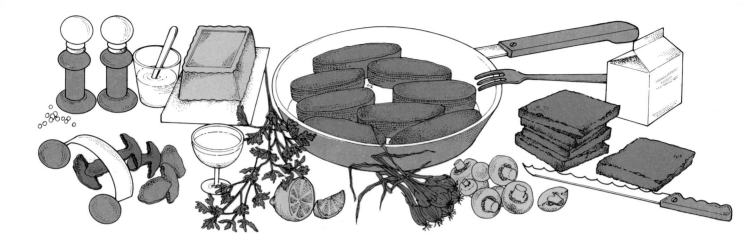

glaze with melted butter and place one on top of each veal steak. Place a little chopped parsley in the center of each mushroom cap. Cut the crusts off the bread, dry out the slices in the oven and keep them warm until required. Place the butter, chopped mushrooms and shallot in a frying pan and sauté briefly. Season the veal lightly with salt and pepper then brown lightly on both sides; pour in the Armagnac, heat and flame. Remove the veal from the pan, drain and place each steak on a slice of crisped bread; keep warm. Add the diluted meat essence/extract and the cream to the juices in the pan, boil for a few minutes to reduce the sauce slightly; add the lemon juice and pour a little sauce over each veal steak. Garnish with glazed mushroom caps.

Preparation: 20 minutes.

MENU 67

Avocado fool
Guinea fowl with Champagne
Creamed potatoes
Buttered spinach
White Lady sundae

Shopping list

1 guinea fowl (preferably a hen) ● 1 small carton whipping cream ● 9 fl oz/250 ml light/single cream ● 2 eggs ● 1 small can pineapple rings ● 1 small can peach halves ● 2 avocados ● 1 onion ● 1 tomato ● small bunch parsley ● 1 lemon ● 1 can or packet instant creamed potatoes ● 1 lb/450 g frozen spinach ● 1 small can or bottle sweet peppers ● ½ bottle Champagne or sparkling white wine ● 11 oz/300 g vanilla ice cream ● 1 small jar apricot jam.

From the store cupboard ● butter – shallot – flour – bay leaf – brandy – Worcestershire sauce – Tabasco sauce – paprika – Grand Marnier – salt – pepper.

Work schedule ● Start cooking the guinea fowl. Make the avocado fool and chill in the refrigerator. Prepare the buttered spinach and creamed potatoes. Make the White Lady sundae.

Avocado fool

2 ripe avocados
1 tbsp finely chopped onion

4 tbsp unsweetened whipped cream
1 tbsp brandy
1 tbsp finely diced canned or bottled pepper
1 tbsp finely diced tomato, seeded and skinned
1 tbsp lemon juice
a few drops Worcestershire sauce
a few drops Tabasco sauce
1 tsp paprika
salt

Cut the avocados in half lengthwise, discard the stones and scoop out the flesh; place in a bowl and mash coarsely with a fork. Stir in all the other ingredients, with the exception of the paprika, and fill the empty avocado skins with the mixture. Sprinkle with paprika and chill in the refrigerator for 30 minutes.

Preparation: 15 minutes.

Guinea fowl with Champagne

1 guinea fowl
salt

pepper
¼ cup/2 oz/50 g butter
2 tbsp finely chopped onion
1 tbsp finely chopped shallot
½ bottle Champagne or sparkling white wine
1 tbsp butter and 2 tbsp flour, cooked together to make a roux
1 bay leaf
1½ cups/9 fl oz/250 ml light/single cream
2 egg yolks

Use a cleaver or poultry scissors to divide the guinea fowl into 8 pieces; season with salt and pepper and place in a heavy-bottomed saucepan with the butter, onion and shallot. Cover tightly and cook over a low heat for 20 minutes, turning the portions from time to time so that they do not burn. Remove the lid, turn up the heat and pour in the Champagne. Allow to boil for a few minutes then add a little of this liquid to the roux. Stir to soften the roux and then add to the saucepan together with the bay leaf. Continue cooking until the guinea fowl is tender and completely cooked. Remove the portions from the pan and keep warm. Add half the cream to the pan and boil fast until the sauce is reduced to half its volume. Remove from the heat and skim off excess fat from the surface; mix the egg yolks with the remaining cream and pour into the sauce. Return the pan to a very low heat and cook gently, stirring continuously until the sauce thickens slightly. Take a large, oval heated serving platter and arrange a border of buttered spinach around the edge of half the platter and a border of creamed potato around the other half. Place the guinea fowl portions in the center and

moisten with one or two spoonfuls of the sauce. Serve the remaining sauce separately.

Preparation: 50 minutes.

White Lady sundae

scant 2 cups/11 oz/300 g vanilla ice cream
4 canned pineapple rings
4 canned peach halves
6/4 tbsp apricot sauce (heat apricot jam and water, stir in 1 tbsp Grand Marnier and sieve)

Chill the sundae dishes well in advance; place a couple of scoops of ice cream in each and place a pineapple ring and half a peach on top. Pour over the apricot sauce and serve.

Preparation: 10 minutes.

MENU 68

Ribbon noodles with butter and sage
Venison steaks with cream and brandy sauce
Peas with butter
Meringues Negrita

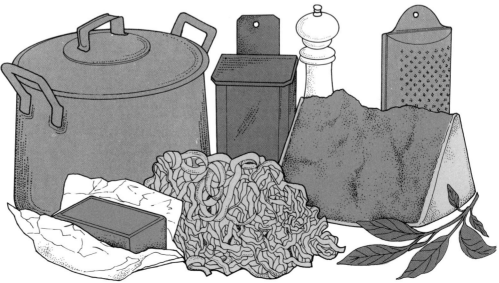

14 oz/400 g ribbon noodles (tagliatelle) ● 1¼ lb/600 g venison steaks (fillet or upper leg/haunch) ● 9 fl oz/250 ml whipping cream ● 1 small carton sour cream ● 3½ oz/100 g freshly grated Parmesan cheese ● 1 packet frozen peas ● fresh sage ● small bunch parsley ● 8 meringues ● 2 oz/50 g cocoa powder ● 2 oz/50 g chocolate hundreds-and-thousands.

From the store cupboard ● butter – meat essence/extract – flour – vanilla flavoured confectioners'/icing sugar – brandy – 1 lemon – salt – pepper – Worcestershire sauce – clarified butter (p. 11).

Work schedule ● Whip the cream and leave in a cool place. Start cooking the venison. Boil the ribbon noodles and while they are cooking, prepare the buttered peas.

Ribbon noodles with butter and sage

14 oz/400 g ribbon noodles (tagliatelle)
salt
½ cup/4 oz/125 g butter
3 fresh sage leaves
½ tsp meat essence/extract dissolved in ½ cup/
4 fl oz/125 ml hot water
pepper
⅓ cup/3 oz/80 g freshly grated Parmesan cheese

Put the ribbon noodles on to cook in a large pan of fast boiling salted water. Melt the butter in a small saucepan with the sage leaves and sauté very gently. After a few minutes remove and discard the sage leaves; pour the diluted meat essence/extract into the saucepan, add freshly ground pepper and boil for a few minutes to reduce the liquid. When the noodles are tender (7-10 minutes), drain well and turn into a heated serving dish; cover with the sauce and sprinkle with half the grated cheese. Mix and serve at once. Serve the remaining cheese separately.

Preparation: 10 minutes.

Venison steaks with cream and brandy sauce

1¼ lb/600 g venison steaks, from the fillet or upper leg/haunch
salt
pepper
1 tbsp flour
2 tbsp clarified butter
6/4 tbsp brandy
⅔ cup/5 fl oz/150 ml sour cream
a few drops lemon juice
a few drops Worcestershire sauce
½ tbsp chopped parsley

Remove any membrane or gristle from the meat before pounding flat with a meat bat. Season with salt and pepper, coat lightly with flour and brown on both sides in the clarified butter over a high heat. Pour in the brandy and set alight. As soon as it has flamed, remove the venison slices. Add the cream to the juices and butter in the pan and boil until the liquid is reduced by half. Add the lemon juice, Worcestershire sauce and chopped parsley; return the venison steaks to the pan and turn them so that they absorb the sauce. Transfer the steaks to a heated serving dish; pour over the sauce and serve.

Preparation: 20 minutes.

Meringues Negrita

8 meringues, homemade or bought
1½ cups/9 fl oz/250 ml whipping cream
2 tbsp vanilla flavoured confectioners'/icing sugar
1 tbsp unsweetened cocoa powder
1 tbsp chocolate hundreds-and-thousands

Whip the cream and add the vanilla flavoured confectioners'/icing sugar gradually. Sift the cocoa powder and fold in carefully; sandwich the meringues together with a generous quantity

of chocolate whipped cream and arrange on a serving plate. Sprinkle with the chocolate hundreds-and-thousands.

Preparation: 10 minutes.

MENU 69

**Cheese-filled pancakes
Ham and sausages with
sauerkraut**
Boiled potatoes
Peaches Alexandra

Shopping list

1 14-oz/400-g piece smoked ham ● 4 small sausages (Frankfurters, Vienna sausages or Bockwurst) ● ¾ lb/350 g Fontina Valdostana cheese (or Emmental) ● 2 eggs ● 2¼ lb/1 kg potatoes ● 9 fl oz/250 ml light/single cream ● 9 fl oz/250 ml canned cream of celery soup ● 1¾ lb/800 g canned sauerkraut ● 1 small jar strawberry jam ● 1 small bottle Melba sauce ● 1 medium can peaches ● 2 oz/50 g toasted flaked almonds ● 1 sponge cake.

From the store cupboard ● milk – Parmesan cheese – flour – nutmeg – sugar – Grand Marnier – salt – pepper.

Work schedule ● Make the pancakes and leave ready to be placed in the oven. Set the potatoes to boil. Heat the smoked ham, sausages and sauerkraut, then prepare the Peaches Alexandra.

Cheese-filled pancakes

generous 1 cup/9 fl oz/250 ml canned cream of celery soup (or equal quantity white sauce)
generous 1 cup/9 fl oz/250 ml light/single cream
pinch grated nutmeg
pepper
¾ lb/350 g Fontina Valdostana cheese (or Emmental), diced
8 pancakes (see p. 30)
a knob of butter
3/2 tbsp freshly grated Parmesan cheese

Mix the cold celery soup or white sauce and the cream together with the nutmeg and pepper; add one-quarter of this mixture to the diced cheese in a bowl and stir with a wooden spoon, until the cheese is well coated. Place an equal amount of this mixture in each of the pancakes, fold two edges inwards and then roll up the pancakes. Butter a wide, fairly shallow ovenproof dish, spoon a little of the seasoned celery soup and cream over the bottom and arrange the rolled pancakes in a single layer. Pour the remaining cream over them and sprinkle with grated Parmesan cheese. Bake in a preheated oven at 450°F/230°C/mk 8 for 12 minutes and then serve immediately.

Preparation (with ready-made pancakes): 8 minutes, otherwise 25 minutes.
Total time: 40 minutes.

Opposite:
Menu 56, page 86

Ham and sausages with sauerkraut

1³/₄ lb/800 g canned sauerkraut
1 14-oz/400-g piece smoked ham, cut into four
4 small sausages (Frankfurters, Vienna sausages or Bockwurst)

Heat the sauerkraut according to the manufacturer's instructions. Place the ham on top of the sauerkraut to warm through. Heat a saucepan of lightly salted water to boiling point, turn off the heat and add the sausages; leave them in the hot water until they have warmed through (never boil). Transfer the sauerkraut to a heated serving dish and place the sausages and the smoked ham on top.

Preparation: 15 minutes.

Peaches Alexandra

1 small sponge cake

4/3 tbsp sugar syrup (half sugar, half water, boiled together until the sugar has totally dissolved)
1 tbsp Grand Marnier
4 tsp strawberry jam
4 canned peach halves
4/3 tbsp Melba sauce
1 tbsp toasted flaked almonds

Cut the sponge cake horizontally in half and use a pastry cutter to cut out circles the same diameter as the peach halves. Place a sponge circle in each sundae dish and sprinkle with a mixture of the sugar syrup and Grand Marnier. Place 1 tsp strawberry jam in the center of each sponge circle and cover with a peach half, rounded side up. Spoon a little Melba sauce over each peach and decorate with toasted almonds.

Preparation: 10 minutes.

MENU 70

Consommé Célestine
Quails with olives
Spinach purée and creamed potatoes
Assorted cheeses

Shopping list

8 quails • 4 spicy sausages • 8 very thin slices salt bacon/belly of pork • 1 egg • 1 can chicken consommé (4 servings) • 7 oz/200 g pitted black olives • 1 packet frozen spinach • 1 can or packet instant creamed potatoes • 1 small carton light/single cream • small bunch parsley • the following selection of herbs: chervil, tarragon, chives, fresh sage, rosemary, bay leaves.

From the store cupboard • butter – flour – nutmeg – milk – dry white wine – meat essence/extract – stock – onion – clarified butter (see p. 11) – salt – pepper.

Work schedule • Make the two pancakes. Prepare the quails for cooking. Start the Consommé Célestine. Cook the quails and while they are cooking, make the spinach purée and creamed potatoes.

Opposite:
Menu 59, page 92

Consommé Célestine

1 can chicken consommé (4 servings)
2 thin pancakes, cut into thin strips
1 level tbsp finely chopped parsley
nutmeg
1 tbsp finely chopped fresh herbs (chervil, tarragon and chives) or, if these are unavailable fresh, substitute 1 tbsp finely chopped parsley

Make the pancakes according to the method on page 30, adding 1 level tbsp finely chopped parsley and a pinch grated nutmeg to the batter. Cut the pancakes into very narrow strips. Gently heat the consommé containing the strips of pancake; add the fresh herbs and serve without delay.

Preparation: 20 minutes.

Quails with olives

4 fresh sage leaves
1 cup/7 oz/200 g pitted black olives
4 spicy sausages, skinned and crumbled with a fork
8 quails
salt
pepper
8 very thin slices salt bacon/belly of pork
2 tbsp clarified butter
2 tbsp finely chopped onion
1 sprig rosemary
2 bay leaves
2/3 cup/5 fl oz/150 ml stock mixed with 1/2 tsp meat essence/extract
2/3 cup/5 fl oz/150 ml dry white wine

Place ½ a sage leaf, 2 olives and a little sausage meat inside each quail. Sprinkle with salt and pepper and wrap each bird in a slice of salt bacon/belly of pork. Secure with a wooden cocktail stick. Cook in clarified butter over direct heat in a covered heavy-bottomed pan. After 10 minutes add the finely chopped onion, the rosemary and bay leaves and continue cooking, adding a little stock when necessary to moisten. When the quails are tender, remove the lid, pour in the white wine and add the remaining olives. Cook until the wine has evaporated; remove the quails and set aside to keep warm. Add the remaining stock to the pan and allow to reduce slightly before serving.

Preparation: 35 minutes.

MENU 71

Mussel kebabs
Curried Arabian veal
Plain boiled rice
Fruit salad with kirsch

Shopping list

2¼ lb/1 kg fresh mussels or 1 can mussels in brine (4 servings) • 1¼ lb/600 g thin veal slices, from upper leg or heel of round • 3½ oz/100 g smoked streaky bacon, thinly sliced • 11 oz/300 g risotto rice • a selection of savoury relishes • 9 fl oz/250 ml light/single cream • 1 egg • 1 onion • 2 oranges • 1 peach • 1 small pineapple • 2 apples • 1 lemon • small bunch parsley • mint or lemon balm • 2 oz/50 g toasted flaked almonds • 1 small jar or can cherries.

From the store cupboard • kirsch – cocktail cherries – dry white wine – bay leaf – peppercorns – breadcrumbs – flour – clarified butter (see p. 11) – butter – Tabasco sauce – Worcestershire sauce – salt – pepper – curry powder.

Work schedule • Prepare the fruit salad and chill in the refrigerator. Set out the ingredients for the mussel kebabs and for the veal steaks. Boil the rice and while it is cooking, cook the kebabs and the veal steaks.

Mussel kebabs

2¼ lb/1 kg fresh mussels or 1 can (4 servings)
If fresh mussels are used:
   ½ cup/4 fl oz/125 ml dry white wine
   a few sprigs parsley (with stalks)
   ½ bay leaf
   a few peppercorns

1 egg
freshly toasted fine breadcrumbs
3½ oz/100 g thinly sliced smoked streaky bacon
2½ tbsp/generous 1 oz/30 g butter
a selection of relishes (e.g. tomato, cucumber, chilli, etc.)

Pick over the fresh mussels and discard any with damaged or open shells. Scrub clean and place in a wide frying pan with the wine, parsley, bay leaf and peppercorns. Cover tightly and place over a high heat for a few minutes until the mussels have opened. Discard any which remain closed. Remove the mussels from their shells and pat dry with paper towels. Dip the mussels in the lightly beaten egg and coat with breadcrumbs. Thread the mussels on skewers and wrap a slice of bacon around each skewer. Place in a shallow ovenproof dish, sprinkle with a little melted butter and bake in a preheated oven at 450°F/230°C/mk 8 for a few minutes; remove from the oven when the bacon fat is translucent and has begun to melt. Serve the savoury relishes separately.

Preparation: 10-15 minutes.

Curried Arabian veal

1¼ lb/600 g thin veal slices, from upper leg or heel of round
2 tbsp flour
2 tbsp clarified butter
1 tbsp finely chopped onion
1 tbsp curry powder
½ cup/4 fl oz/125 ml dry white wine
1½ cups/9 fl oz/225 ml light/single cream
salt
pepper
a few drops Tabasco sauce

1 tbsp Worcestershire sauce
2 tbsp toasted flaked almonds
8 canned cherries, pitted

Cut the veal slices into small pieces about 1 in/2.5 cm square. Place in a bowl and coat lightly with flour, mixing with your hands. Heat the clarified butter in a large frying pan until very hot; add the veal and fry quickly over a very high heat, stirring constantly with a wooden spatula. When the veal has browned slightly, remove at once, drain well, and keep warm between two hot plates. Add the chopped onion and curry powder and fry briefly over a moderate heat; pour in the white wine and cook until it has partly evaporated. Add the cream and reduce

by half, boiling steadily. Season with salt, pepper, Tabasco and Worcestershire sauce. Return the veal to the pan and stir so that the meat is well coated with sauce. Remove from the heat, transfer to a heated serving dish and garnish with the toasted flaked almonds and cherries.

Preparation: 15 minutes.

Fruit salad with kirsch

For this colourful fruit salad, choose whatever is available and in season, using the following selection as a guide: melon, grapefruit, oranges, fresh pineapple, apples, peaches and grapes. A small quantity of 4 types of fruit will be sufficient, for example:

2 apples
¼ fresh pineapple
2 oranges

1 peach
juice of ½ lemon
6/4 tbsp kirsch
4 cocktail cherries
8 leaves fresh mint or lemon balm

Peel, core and dice the apples and pineapple. Peel and remove all the pith from the oranges, separate into segments and cut each segment in half. Remove the stone from the peach and dice the flesh. Mix the fruits together, sprinkle with the lemon juice and kirsch and chill in the refrigerator for at least 45 minutes. Spoon the fruit salad into glass sundae dishes or tall goblets and garnish with cocktail cherries and mint or lemon balm leaves.

Preparation: 10 minutes.
Refrigeration: 45 minutes.

MENU 72

Crudités
Hake Colbert
Steamed potatoes
Chippenham cheese savoury

Shopping list

4 7-oz/200-g hake or cod steaks or fillets ● a selection of fresh, crisp vegetables ● 1 bottle best quality olive oil ● oil for deep frying ● 5 oz/150 g Cheddar cheese ● 3 eggs ● small bunch parsley ● 1 lemon ● 1 small carton light/single cream ● 1 loaf of bread.

From the store cupboard ● butter – milk – flour – freshly toasted fine breadcrumbs – salt – pepper – white wine vinegar.

Work schedule ● Place the fish steaks or fillets in milk to soak. Make the Maître d'hôtel butter and chill in the refrigerator. Set the potatoes to steam (see p. 40). Prepare the Crudités. Fry the fish and set out the ingredients for the cheese savoury. Crisp the fingers of bread in the oven.

Crudités

Raw vegetables are extremely nutritious and aid digestion, especially when eaten as part of an evening meal. Choose a variety of fresh, crisp vegetables, such as celery hearts, fennel, radishes, carrots, lettuce, Belgian endive/chicory, red or green peppers, etc. Take care when preparing the vegetables to trim off all tough or discoloured parts; slice into fairly small pieces or strips and arrange in a glass bowl with a little iced water or cracked ice. In front of each guest place a small bowl of vinaigrette dressing, made with best quality white wine vinegar, olive oil, salt and freshly ground pepper.

Preparation: 15 minutes

Hake Colbert

4 7-oz/200-g hake or cod steaks or fillets
generous 1 cup/9 fl oz/250 ml milk
salt
flour
1 egg
5/3 tbsp freshly toasted fine breadcrumbs
oil for deep frying
6 tbsp/3 oz/80 g Maître d'hôtel butter

Soak the fish in salted milk for 20 minutes. Drain, pat dry and season the fish with a little salt. Coat lightly with flour, dip in the lightly beaten egg and then in breadcrumbs before deep frying in plenty of very hot oil. When the fish are crisp and golden brown on the outside, remove carefully with a slotted fish slice and drain well. Serve a large piece of Maître d'hôtel butter with each.

Preparation: 55 minutes.

Maître d'hôtel butter

Mix 6 tbsp/3 oz/80 g softened butter with 1 tsp very finely chopped parsley, a little salt and pepper and a few drops lemon juice. Work well with a fork or wooden spoon then chill in the refrigerator until very firm.

Chippenham cheese savoury

2 egg yolks
scant 1 cup/5 fl oz/150 ml light/single cream
1¼ cups/5 oz/150 g grated Cheddar cheese
slices of bread (crusts removed), cut into fingers and crisped in the oven

This dish provides an informal end to a relaxed dinner party with friends. The cheese, egg and cream mixture is cooked in a double boiler and then placed in the center of the table, either in the same double boiler or in a fondue dish. The idea is much the same as a fondue, each person dipping a finger of bread, speared on the end of a fondue fork, into the creamy cheese mixture. Heat the water in a double boiler very gently. Place the egg yolks in the top part of the double boiler and stir constantly with a wooden spoon as they warm slightly. Add the cream a little at a time, beating constantly. Once all the cream has been added, sprinkle in the grated cheese gradually. The water in the bottom of the double boiler should not boil. Stir the mixture constantly with a wooden spoon as the cheese melts. The mixture should be thick and creamy. The cheese dip should be ready before the water reaches boiling point.

Preparation: 10 minutes.

Salade niçoise
Grilled filet mignon
Sweet and sour onions
Assorted cheeses

Shopping list

4 ¼-lb/125-g loin tenderloin/fillet beef steaks ● 11 oz/300 g flaked tuna fish ● 7 oz/200 g pitted black olives ● 3½ oz/100 g canned anchovy fillets ● 2 eggs ● 2 oz/50 g capers ● assorted cheeses ● 11 oz/300 g canned French beans ● 1 lb/450 g small onions ● 2 large ripe tomatoes ● 2 potatoes ● 1 lemon ● small bunch parsley ● 1 loaf of bread.

From the store cupboard ● butter – wine vinegar – sugar – onion – garlic – tarragon vinegar or fresh tarragon – olive oil – sunflower oil – salt – pepper.

Work schedule ● Cook the potatoes for the Salade niçoise in a pressure cooker; hard-boil the eggs and drain the French beans. Start cooking the Sweet and sour onions and while they are cooking, make the Salade niçoise. Broil/grill the fillet steaks.

Salade niçoise

11 oz/300 g canned French beans
2 large ripe tomatoes
2 cold boiled potatoes, cut into small cubes
½ onion, thinly sliced
1½ cups/11 oz/300 g flaked tuna fish
16-20 pitted black olives, halved
8 anchovy fillets, coarsely chopped
1 tbsp chopped parsley
2 hard-boiled eggs, sliced or quartered
3 slices bread, crusts removed, cut into 1-in/2.5-cm squares, crisped in the oven and rubbed with a clove of garlic
Dressing:
2 tbsp tarragon vinegar (or mix finely chopped fresh tarragon with wine vinegar)
5/3 tbsp olive oil
salt
pepper
Garnish: 1 lemon, cut into wedges and a few sprigs parsley

Boil the potatoes in the pressure cooker and leave to cool. Arrange all the ingredients on a large serving platter, reserving a few pieces of anchovy, olive, tomato, etc., for garnish. Mix the dressing and pour over the salad just before serving. Garnish with the lemon wedges and sprigs of parsley.

Preparation: 30 minutes.

Grilled filet mignon

4 ¼-lb/125-g loin tenderloin/fillet beef steaks
1 tbsp sunflower oil
salt
freshly ground pepper

If the steaks have been cut from the pointed end of the fillet flatten them slightly, pounding not too hard against the grain. If they have been cut from the center of the fillet they will already be thin enough. Season the steaks with salt and pepper and brush lightly with oil on both sides; place under a very hot broiler/grill and cook according to preference, turning once only. If the meat is not to be served immediately, keep warm between two hot plates.

Preparation: 5 minutes.

Sweet and sour onions

1 lb/450 g small onions
3 tbsp/1½ oz/40 g butter
1 tsp sugar
salt
¼ cup/2 fl oz/60 ml vinegar
pepper

Peel the onions and sauté gently in the butter, shaking the pan from time to time so that they cook evenly; when they have started to brown, add the sugar and sprinkle with salt. Fry for a few minutes longer, until the sugar has coloured lightly; add the vinegar and a little water a spoonful at a time. Cover the pan when all the liquid has been added and cook slowly until the onions are tender. Season with pepper shortly before serving.

Preparation: 10 minutes.
Total time: 35 minutes.

MENU 74

Gnocchi Paris style
Veal and bacon kebabs
Peas with butter
Raspberry mousse

Shopping list

1¼ lb/600 g veal cutlets/escalopes or tenderloin/fillet of pork • 3½ oz/100 g thickly sliced salt bacon/belly of pork • 3 oz/80 g rolled Italian pancetta, preferably machine cut into thin slices • 3 eggs • 18 fl oz/500 ml milk • 9 fl oz/250 ml heavy/double cream • 1 packet frozen peas • ½ lb/225 g frozen raspberries • fresh sage leaves • 5 oz/150 g freshly grated Parmesan, Gruyère or Emmental cheese • 7 oz/200 g vanilla ice cream.

From the store cupboard • butter – stock – kirsch – gelatine – flour – sugar – salt – pepper.

Work schedule • Make the Raspberry mousse and chill in the refrigerator; make the Gnocchi and the Mornay sauce. Prepare the kebabs and place the Gnocchi in the oven. Cook the peas and the kebabs.

Gnocchi Paris style

1¼ cups/½ pint/300 ml water
6 tbsp/3 oz/80 g butter
salt
scant 1 cup/scant 4 oz/120 g flour
3 eggs
2¼ cups/18 fl oz/500 ml Mornay sauce (see method)
¼ cup/2 oz/50 g freshly grated Parmesan, Gruyère or Emmental cheese
1 cup/6 fl oz/175 ml heavy/double cream

3 tbsp/1½ oz/40 g butter
salt
pepper
a little stock

Cut the veal or pork into very thin slices and dice the salt bacon/belly of pork. Lay the slices of meat out flat and cover with the thinly sliced pancetta, trimmed to the same size. Place a fresh sage leaf on top and fold the meat in half, with the pancetta on the inside. Thread onto a skewer (allow 4 or 5 veal slices per skewer) and place a cube of salt bacon/belly of pork between each. Fry gently in butter in a large frying pan and season with salt and pepper; drain and keep warm on a serving platter. Add a little stock to the frying pan, boil very briefly and pour the meat juices over the kebabs.

Preparation: 15 minutes.

Raspberry mousse

1 sheet leaf gelatine (or 1 sachet / ½ oz / 15 g powdered gelatine)
½ lb/225 g frozen raspberries
½ cup/4 fl oz/125 ml kirsch
generous 1 cup/7 oz/200 g vanilla ice cream
½ cup/4 fl oz/125 ml sugar syrup (made by boiling equal quantities of sugar and water together)
6/4 tbsp sweetened whipped cream

If leaf gelatine is used, soak in cold water to soften. Place half the raspberries with the kirsch in the blender; liquidize and then add the ice cream, blending in one-third at a time. Squeeze

Place the water, butter and a pinch of salt in a small saucepan; bring to a fast boil and pour in the flour all at once; remove from the heat immediately and beat with a wooden spoon until the mixture is smooth and well blended. Return the pan to a lower heat and stir continuously until the mixture forms a solid ball and begins to sizzle. Transfer to a bowl, mix in the cheese and then work in the eggs one at a time, beating thoroughly before adding the next. Place a wide nozzle in an icing bag and spoon in the gnocchi dough; have a large pan of salted water at a brisk boil and push short lengths of dough through the nozzle, cutting it to drop directly into the boiling water. Remove the gnocchi with a slotted spoon as soon as they rise to the surface and place in a heated buttered ovenproof dish. Do not allow the gnocchi to overcook. Make the Mornay sauce: take 2¼ cups/18 fl oz/500 ml béchamel sauce and stir in 1 cup/6 fl oz/175 ml heavy/double cream and ¼ cup/2 oz/50 g freshly grated Parmesan, Gruyère or Emmental cheese. Heat, stirring continuously, until the cheese has melted and stir in ¼ cup/2 oz/50 g butter. Pour the sauce over the gnocchi and place in a preheated oven at 450°F/230°C/mk 8 until the surface is lightly browned.

Preparation: 25 minutes.
Total time: 45 minutes.

Veal and bacon kebabs

1¼ lb/600 g veal cutlets/escalopes or tenderloin/fillet of pork
3½ oz/100 g thickly sliced salt bacon/belly of pork
3 oz/80 g rolled Italian pancetta, preferably machine cut into thin slices
fresh sage

the gelatine to get rid of excess water and dissolve in the hot sugar syrup (or soften powdered gelatine with a little cold water and then dissolve in the hot, not boiling, sugar syrup) and add to the ice cream mixture. Blend well. Divide the remaining raspberries between four sundae dishes, reserving four for decoration. Pour the mixture from the liquidizer over the raspberries and chill in the refrigerator. Top each dessert with sweetened whipped cream and a whole raspberry just before serving.

Preparation: 15 minutes.
Refrigeration: 45 minutes.

MENU 75

Risotto with scampi and brandy
Spring chicken with white wine
Mixed salad
Oranges in Triple Sec

Shopping list

2 2-lb/900-g oven-ready spring chickens ● 11 oz/300 g scampi or shrimp/prawns ● 14 oz/400 g risotto rice ● 1 anchovy fillet ● 1 egg ● 4 oranges ● mixed salad ingredients ● small bunch parsley ● fresh sage leaves ● rosemary.

From the store cupboard ● butter – oil – wine vinegar – Triple Sec (or Curaçao) – sugar – onion – dry white wine – stock – chilli pepper – garlic – brandy – salt – pepper – bay leaf.

Work schedule ● Place the chickens in the oven to roast. Wash and drain the salad. Peel and slice the oranges, sprinkle with Triple Sec and chill in the refrigerator. Prepare the scampi sauce for the risotto. Cook the rice.

Risotto with scampi and brandy

½ tbsp chopped onion
6 tbsp/3 oz/80 g butter
2 cups/14 oz/400 g risotto rice
⅔ cup/5 fl oz/150 ml dry white wine
1 bay leaf
4½ cups/1¾ pints/1 liter light stock
½ anchovy fillet
1 small piece chilli pepper
½ clove garlic
2 tbsp oil
1¾ cups/11 oz/300 g scampi or shrimp/prawns
salt
pepper
4/3 tbsp brandy
1 tsp finely chopped parsley
1 egg yolk

Sauté the onion in 2½ tbsp/generous 1 oz/30 g butter until translucent; add the rice and cook briefly, stirring to coat each grain with butter. Pour in half the wine and allow to evaporate; add the bay leaf and half the boiling stock. Cook for about 18 minutes or until the rice is tender but still firm, adding more boiling stock as the risotto absorbs the liquid. Meanwhile, finely chop the anchovy fillet, chilli pepper and garlic and sauté in oil; add the scampi, season with a little salt and pepper and cook over a fairly low heat for 2-3 minutes. Pour in the remaining wine and allow to evaporate. Set aside to keep warm if the risotto is not yet ready. Return the scampi to the heat and add the brandy and parsley. When the risotto is nearly ready, add half the scampi and mix carefully. Remove the risotto from the heat while it is still quite moist. Add the remaining butter, cut into small pieces, and the egg yolk; stir vigorously with a wooden spatula to give the risotto a glossy finish. Transfer to a heated serving dish and top with the remaining scampi.

Preparation: 35 minutes.

Spring chicken with white wine

2 sprigs fresh sage
2 sprigs rosemary
2 2-lb/900-g oven-ready spring chickens
salt
pepper
5 tbsp/2½ oz/60 g melted butter
⅔ cup/5 fl oz/150 ml dry white wine

Place a sprig of sage and rosemary inside each
bird and season with salt and freshly ground
pepper. Truss the chickens and place in a large
roasting pan; brush with melted butter and roast
in a preheated oven at 375°F/190°C/mk 5. When
the chickens have begun to brown, baste with
the white wine and continue roasting for a
further 50-55 minutes, turning from time to
time.

Preparation: 8-10 minutes.
Total time: 1 hour.

MENU 76

Baked avocados
**Stuffed fillet of beef Russian
style**
Bananas in butter
Creamed spinach
Almond torte

Shopping list

11 oz/300 g loin tenderloin/fillet of beef ● 5-7 oz/150-200 g
canned crabmeat ● 9 fl oz/250 ml milk ● 1 large carton
light/single cream ● tomato paste ● 3½ oz/100 g fine semolina
● 1 packet frozen spinach ● 1 small carton sour cream ● 1
lemon ● 2 avocados ● 2 onions ● 4 bananas ● 1 almond torte.

From the store cupboard ● butter – oil – vinegar
– nutmeg – sugar – pepper – curry powder.

Work schedule ● Cook the semolina and make

the white sauce. Place the avocados in the oven
and prepare the beef for cooking. While the
beef is simmering, cook the spinach (see p. 16)
and the bananas.

Baked avocados

generous 1 cup/9 fl oz/250 ml white sauce
1 tsp tomato paste
½ tsp finely chopped onion
1 tbsp melted butter

½ tsp curry powder
1 cup/5-7 oz/150-200 g canned crabmeat
2 avocados
1 lemon
salt

Make the white sauce, remove from the heat and stir in the tomato paste, the onion, melted butter, curry powder and flaked crabmeat. Return to the heat and warm through without boiling. Cut the avocados in half and discard the stones; cut into the flesh in a criss-cross pattern and sprinkle with lemon juice and salt. Spoon the white sauce and crabmeat mixture into the center of each avocado and place in a wide ovenproof dish. Pour water into the bottom of the dish to reach ¾ in/2 cm up the sides; cover the avocados with foil. Bake in a preheated oven at 325°F/170°C/mk 3 for 20 minutes.

Preparation: 40 minutes.

Stuffed fillet of beef Russian style

½ cup/3½ oz/100 g fine semolina
3/2 tbsp very finely chopped onion
3 tbsp/1½ oz/40 g butter
salt
pepper
11 oz/300 g tenderloin/fillet of beef, very thinly sliced
½ cup/4 fl oz/125 ml stock
generous ½ cup/5 fl oz/150 ml sour or fresh cream
creamed spinach (see p. 16)
4 bananas

Cook the semolina in lightly salted water for 20 minutes; when cooked it should not be too moist. Meanwhile, fry the chopped onion in a little butter, then mix with the semolina; season with salt and pepper. Pound the slices of beef with a meat bat into rectangles 5 × 3 in/12 × 8 cm. Spread a little semolina mixture on each slice, roll up and secure with a wooden cocktail stick. Brown the beef rolls in butter and pour in the stock: cover and simmer over a low heat for 15 minutes. When the beef is tender, add the cream and bring almost to boiling point. Prepare the creamed spinach and the bananas separately (see below). Arrange the spinach in a ring around the edge of the serving dish and place the bananas (sliced lengthwise in half and cooked in butter) on top. Place the beef rolls in the center of the serving dish.

Preparation: 10 minutes.
Total time: 50 minutes.

Bananas in butter

Peel the bananas and slice lengthwise in half. Melt a little butter in a frying pan. Fry the bananas briskly, flat side up, for about 30 seconds, turn and fry over a low heat for 1 minute. Bananas prepared in this way are delicious with creamed spinach; arrange the bananas on top of the spinach in a criss-cross pattern or, if served on a circular serving dish, arranged like the spokes of a wheel.

Preparation: 5 minutes.

MENU 77

Creole Jambalaya
Carpaccio
(savoury raw beef)
Mixed green salad
Baked Alaska

Shopping list

1lb/450 g tenderloin/fillet of beef, sliced wafer thin ● 1 small can peppers ● 5 oz/150 g fresh sausages ● 1 3½-oz/100-g slice cooked ham ● 14 oz/400 g risotto rice ● 1 small jar mayonnaise ● 4 eggs ● garlic ● 1 large onion ● small bunch parsley ● Parmesan cheese, ungrated (optional) ● mixed salad ingredients ● 2 lemons ● 1 rectangular sponge cake ● 12 oz/350 g ice cream.

From the store cupboard ● butter – oil – bay leaf – oregano – thyme – stock – cayenne pepper – mustard powder – Worcestershire sauce – salt – superfine/caster sugar.

Work schedule ● Sprinkle salt and lemon juice over the wafer-thin slices of beef and prepare the sauce. Cook the Jambalaya and whisk the egg whites for the Baked Alaska.

Creole Jambalaya

5 oz/150 g fresh sausages
5/3 tbsp oil
1 3½-oz/100-g slice cooked ham, diced
2 cloves garlic, finely chopped
1 large onion, finely chopped
2½ tbsp/generous 1 oz/30 g butter

2 cups/14 oz/400 g risotto rice
1 canned pepper, cut into strips
a chopped mixture of:
   1/2 bay leaf
   1 sprig oregano (or a pinch dried)
   1 sprig thyme
   1 clove garlic
4 1/4 cups/1 3/4 pints/1 liter stock
cayenne pepper
1 tbsp finely chopped parsley

Crumble the sausages and fry gently in half the oil with the diced ham and the chopped garlic. Sauté the onion separately in a large, heavy-bottomed pan in the remaining oil and the butter; add the rice and stir for a minute or two: add the sausage, ham and garlic mixture, the pepper, the chopped mixed herbs and garlic and half the boiling stock. Cook for a further 15-20 minutes, adding more stock as the rice absorbs the liquid (pour in a small quantity at a time). Just before serving, season with cayenne pepper and sprinkle with chopped parsley. Jambalaya should be very moist, not as dry as pilaf rice or Paella.

Preparation: 45 minutes.

Carpaccio (savoury raw beef)

1 lb/450 g tenderloin/fillet of beef, sliced wafer thin
4/3 tbsp lemon juice
3/2 tbsp mayonnaise
1 tsp mustard powder mixed with a little water
a few drops Worcestershire sauce

salt
finely chopped parsley
slices of Parmesan cheese (optional)

Arrange the slices of raw beef on individual plates and sprinkle with salt and lemon juice. Make a sauce by combining the mayonnaise, mustard and Worcestershire sauce and pour over each serving. Sprinkle with chopped parsley. Serve with wafer-thin slices of Parmesan cheese (optional).

Preparation: 5 minutes.

Baked Alaska

4 egg whites
4/3 tbsp superfine/caster sugar
2 cups/12 oz/350 g ice cream, frozen very solid
1 rectangular sponge cake, crusts removed, 1 in/
2 cm thick

Place the sponge cake on a baking sheet. Whisk the egg whites until stiff, gradually adding 3/2 tbsp superfine/caster sugar. Place the ice cream in a solid block on the sponge cake and quickly mask completely with a thick covering of sweetened egg white (use a large icing bag and wide fluted nozzle or a palette knife). Sprinkle the surface lightly with the remaining sugar and bake in a very hot preheated oven (450°F/230°C/ mk 8) for 2 minutes, or until the meringue is golden brown. Serve immediately.

Preparation: 10 minutes.

MENU 78

Tortellini with cheese sauce
Trout Caprice
Mixed salad
Coffee ice cream dessert

Shopping list

4 7-oz/200-g trout ● fresh or vacuum packed tortellini (4 servings) ● 7 oz/200 g canned tomatoes ● 18 fl oz/500 ml milk ● 1 small carton light/single cream ● 4 oz/125 g freshly grated Parmesan cheese ● 2 oz/50 g capers ● small bunch parsley ● 1 lemon ● mixed salad ingredients ● 1 coffee ice cream dessert.

From the store cupboard ● butter – flour – nutmeg – oil – dry white wine – garlic – salt – pepper – wine vinegar.

Work schedule ● Make the white sauce and the tomato sauce for the trout. Wash and drain the salad. Boil the tortellini, cover with the sauce and place in the oven. Cook the trout.

Tortellini with cheese sauce

fresh or vacuum packed tortellini (4 servings)
½ cup/4 oz/125 g freshly grated Parmesan cheese
¼ cup/2 oz/50 g butter
1¼ cups/½ pint/300 ml white sauce
¾ cup/4 fl oz/125 ml light/single cream

Boil the tortellini until tender (5-7 minutes) in plenty of salted water; drain well and arrange in an ovenproof dish. Sprinkle with half the freshly grated Parmesan cheese and small pieces of butter. Heat the white sauce and stir in the cream. Pour the sauce evenly over the tortellini, sprinkle the surface with the remaining Parmesan cheese and dot with small flakes of butter. Place in a very hot oven (450°F/230°C/mk 8) for a few minutes until the top is golden brown.

Preparation: 10 minutes.
Total time: 40 minutes.

Trout Caprice

1 clove garlic, crushed but left whole
3 tbsp/1½ oz/40 g butter
¼ cup/2½ fl oz/75 ml dry white wine
1 cup/7 oz/200 g canned tomatoes, sieved
1 tbsp chopped capers
1 tbsp chopped parsley
salt
pepper
4 7-oz/200-g trout, gutted
½ tbsp lemon juice
flour
2 tbsp oil

Sauté the crushed garlic clove in butter until pale golden brown; remove and discard. Pour in the wine and allow to evaporate; add the sieved tomatoes, chopped capers, parsley and a little salt and pepper; simmer until the sauce has thickened. Sprinkle the trout inside and out with lemon juice and salt and pepper; coat lightly with flour and fry gently in hot oil. Turn the fish when they are half-cooked and pour in the tomato and caper sauce. Simmer gently until the fish are cooked.

Preparation: 20 minutes.
Total time: 50 minutes.

MENU 79

Taramasalata
Fleuret à la Riche
Pilaf rice
Irinka
(Russian sweet chestnut and rum dessert)

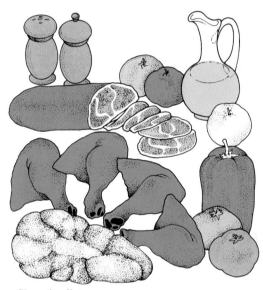

Shopping list

4 chicken legs • 1 calf's kidney • 14 oz/400 g veal sirloin/fillet of veal, cut into ½-in/1-cm slices • 11 oz/300 g long grain rice • 3½ oz/100 g smoked cod's roe • 3½ oz/100 g green olives, pitted • 4 slices smoked bacon, ½ in/1 cm thick • 1 bottle barbecue sauce • 2 red or green peppers • 4 small tomatoes • small bunch parsley • 1 onion • 1 can chestnut purée • 1 small carton whipping cream • 2 oz/50 g toasted almonds • 1 jar preserved ginger.

From the store cupboard • butter – fresh breadcrumbs – brandy – rum – cocktail cherries – oil – paprika – stock – salt.

Work schedule • Prepare the Irinka dessert and chill in the refrigerator. Make the Taramasalata and place in the refrigerator. Start the pilaf rice (see p. 29) and broil/grill the meat.

Taramasalata

3½ oz/100 g smoked cod's roe

1 cup/3½ oz/100 g fresh white breadcrumbs, soaked in water and squeezed free of excess moisture
1 tbsp finely chopped parsley
1 tbsp onion, very finely chopped
½ cup/4 fl oz/125 ml olive oil
green olives for garnish

Place the cod's roe in a bowl with the breadcrumbs, onion and parsley and blend together with a wooden spoon; add the oil a little at a time, working in well after each addition. Chill in the refrigerator and serve garnished with pitted green olives.

Preparation: 15 minutes.

Fleuret à la Riche

4 slices smoked bacon, ½ in/1 cm thick
14 oz/400 g veal sirloin/fillet of veal, cut into ½-in/1-cm slices
2 red or green peppers
1 calf's kidney
4 chicken legs
4 small tomatoes
oil
salt
freshly ground pepper
paprika
5/3 tbsp brandy
barbecue sauce

Cut the bacon, veal, peppers and kidney into small pieces of equal size; brush all the pieces, the chicken legs and tomatoes with oil; season with salt and pepper and a little paprika. Broil/grill, preferably over a charcoal fire, without threading the ingredients on to skewers. Once they are cooked, thread the various meats

Irinka
(Russian sweet chestnut and rum dessert)

1 can chestnut purée
generous ½ cup/5 fl oz/150 ml stiffly whipped
cream
2 tbsp rum
1 tbsp preserved ginger, very finely chopped
½ cup/2 oz/50 g chopped toasted almonds
cocktail cherries

Mix the first four ingredients together and chill in the refrigerator for as long as possible. Decorate with the chopped toasted almonds and cocktail cherries.

Preparation: 5 minutes.

and peppers on a skewer, alternating the different ingredients, and place a tomato on the end of each skewer. Heat the brandy, pour over the mixed grill and flame. Serve each guest one chicken leg and a selection of the grill. Serve the pilaf rice and barbecue sauce separately.

Preparation: 30 minutes.

MENU 80

Avocado and grapefruit starter
Singapore kebabs with Chinese fried rice
Individual rum babas with ice cream

Shopping list

1 lb/450 g cooked ham (shoulder cut), sliced 1 in/2.5 cm thick ● 11 oz/300 g long grain rice ● 1 2-oz/50-g jar shrimp/prawns ● 1 4-oz/125-g packet frozen peas ● 2 avocados ● 3 small grapefruit ● mint or lemon balm ● 1 lemon ● 1 scallion/spring onion or 1 leek ● 2 eggs ● 4 individual rum babas ● 1 small fresh pineapple (or canned) ● 4 portions vanilla ice cream.

From the store cupboard ● cocktail cherries – oil – Tabasco sauce – soy sauce – clarified butter (see p. 11) – salt – rum.

Work schedule ● Marinate the kebabs. Prepare the starter and chill in the refrigerator. Cook the rice and the peas. Finish the Chinese fried rice and fry the Singapore kebabs.

Avocado and grapefruit starter

2 avocados
juice of ½ lemon
3 small grapefruit
8 leaves fresh mint or lemon balm
4 cocktail cherries

Peel the avocados and cut lengthwise in half; discard the stone and slice the flesh evenly. Arrange the slices, overlapping slightly, on small individual plates and sprinkle with lemon juice to prevent discolouration. Peel the grapefruit and divide into segments, removing the inner skin but keeping the segments intact; arrange the segments decoratively around the avocado slices. Garnish with mint or lemon balm leaves and cocktail cherries.

Preparation: 15-20 minutes.

Singapore kebabs

3 slices fresh pineapple (or unsweetened canned)
1 lb/450 g cooked ham (shoulder cut), sliced 1 in/2.5 cm thick
2 tbsp soy sauce
10 drops Tabasco sauce
½ tsp lemon juice
½ cup/4 oz/125 g clarified butter
4 portions Chinese fried rice

Cut each pineapple slice into 6-8 pieces and thread on to the skewers, alternating with the cubes of ham. Place the skewers in a wide dish; mix the soy sauce, Tabasco sauce and lemon juice and sprinkle over the kebabs. Leave to marinate for at least 30 minutes. Fry in butter for 12 minutes, turning several times. Remove the kebabs from the pan, drain and serve on a bed of Chinese fried rice. Do not serve the juices from the pan.

Preparation: 50 minutes.

Chinese fried rice

1½ cups/11 oz/300 g long grain rice
salt
½ cup/2 oz/50 g frozen peas
¼ cup/2 oz/50 g cooked ham, finely diced
½ tbsp chopped scallion/spring onion or leek (green part only)
3/2 tbsp oil
⅓ cup/2 oz/50 g canned shrimp/prawns
2 eggs
1 tbsp soy sauce

Boil the rice in plenty of salted water: drain, rinse with boiling water and spread out immediately on a large plate to cool. Cook the peas until tender; drain. Fry the ham and scallion/spring onion in the oil, add the shrimp/prawns and fry very briefly. Add the rice and fry over a high heat, stirring continuously, for 3-4 minutes. Stir the eggs to break the yolks and pour over the rice. Stir gently before adding the peas and the soy sauce. Serve immediately.

Preparation: 15 minutes, excluding time for cooking the rice.

Individual rum babas with ice cream

4 individual rum babas
6/4 tbsp rum
4 portions vanilla ice cream

Heat a small saucepan, place the babas inside and pour the rum over them. Heat the babas through, spooning over the warm rum with a long-handled spoon. Set the hot rum alight and flame. Serve the ice cream on individual plates with one rum baba per guest; sprinkle the remaining hot rum over the dessert.

Preparation: 5 minutes.

MENU 81

Clam chowder
**Chinese sweet and sour pork
(T'ang Ts'u P'ai Ku)**
Boiled rice
Fruit and cheese salad
Assorted cheeses or fresh fruit

Opposite:
Menu 65, page 100

Shopping list

1 lb/450 g lean pork ● 1 can clam chowder (4 servings) ● 1 jar Chinese mixed pickles in sweet and sour sauce ● 1 jar mayonnaise ● 1 anchovy fillet ● 5 oz/150 g Bel Paese cheese ● 11 oz/300 g rice ● 1 grapefruit ● 1 orange ● 1 banana ● 1 scallion/spring onion ● assorted cheeses or fresh fruit ● 1 lettuce ● small bunch parsley.

From the store cupboard ● dry sherry – flour – cornstarch/cornflour – sugar – wine vinegar – garlic – chilli pepper – oil – dry white wine – salt – pepper – monosodium glutamate (optional).

Work schedule ● Leave the pork cubes to marinate. Prepare the salad. Set the rice to boil and fry the pork. Sauté the chopped garnish for the Clam Chowder and heat the soup.

Clam chowder

To accentuate the flavour of the clam chowder add the following chopped ingredients:

1 anchovy fillet
1 clove garlic
¼ chilli pepper
a little parsley

Chop the above ingredients very finely and sauté in 2 tbsp oil; pour in ¼ cup/2 fl oz/60 ml dry white wine and boil until reduced by half. Add to the clam chowder while it is heating.

Preparation: 15 minutes.

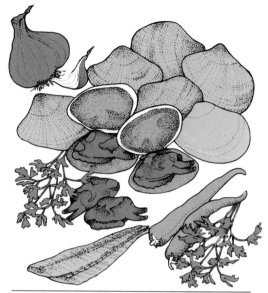

Chinese sweet and sour pork
(T'ang Ts'u P'ai Ku)

1 lb/450 g lean pork, cut into small cubes
salt
pepper
monosodium glutamate (optional)
1 tsp dry sherry
4 tbsp/1 oz/25 g cornstarch/cornflour
4/3 tbsp soy sauce
oil for frying
2 tbsp oil
1 scallion/spring onion, thinly sliced
¼ clove garlic, crushed
2 tbsp sugar
6/4 tbsp Chinese mixed pickles in sweet and sour sauce
3/2 tbsp vinegar
6/4 tbsp water
4 portions plain boiled rice

Season the pork cubes with salt, pepper, a pinch monosodium glutamate, sherry, half the cornstarch/cornflour and half the soy sauce. Mix well and leave to marinate. Deep fry the pork in batches until cooked through and crisp on the outside. Drain well and keep hot. Heat 2 tbsp oil in a frying pan and sauté the sliced scallion/spring onion and the crushed but still whole piece of garlic very lightly; remove the garlic and discard. Add the sugar, the remaining soy sauce, Chinese mixed pickles and the vinegar; bring to the boil, stir in the remaining cornstarch/cornflour mixed with the water, and cook for a few minutes, stirring constantly. Remove from the heat and pour over the pork. Serve the plain boiled rice separately.

Opposite:
Menu 79, page 121

N.B. To keep the boiled rice grains separate, turn the cooked rice into a sieve, drain quickly and rinse with boiling water.

Preparation: 35 minutes.

Fruit and cheese salad

1 orange
1 grapefruit
1 banana
pinch superfine/caster sugar
5 oz/150 g Bel Paese cheese
plenty of freshly ground pepper

1 lettuce
a little oil and wine vinegar
4/3 tbsp mayonnaise

Peel the orange and grapefruit; remove each segment intact from its inner skin and mix with the thinly sliced banana. Sweeten slightly. Dice the Bel Paese cheese and roll in plenty of freshly ground pepper; mix with the lettuce torn into small pieces and dress with a mixture of oil and vinegar. Stir carefully into the fruit and add the mayonnaise last of all.

Preparation: 15 minutes.

MENU 82

Shrimp/prawns Tourkolimano (Greek style)
Cantonese fried chicken
Boiled rice
Banana dessert

Shopping list

2 2-lb/900-g oven-ready chickens ● 3 oz/80 g Feta (Greek cheese) ● 11 oz/300 g raw shrimp/prawns (fresh or frozen) ● 11 oz/300 g long grain rice ● 1 lb/450 g canned tomatoes ● 1 onion ● 2 scallions/spring onions ● 4 ripe bananas ● 4 portions vanilla ice cream.

From the store cupboard ● butter – olive oil – brandy – Ouzo, anisette or Pernod – garlic – soy sauce – flour – oil for frying – sherry – chicken stock – cornstarch/cornflour – sugar – banana cream liqueur or maraschino liqueur – rum – salt – pepper – ground cinnamon – ground ginger.

Work schedule ● Joint the chickens, cutting each into 8 pieces, and leave to marinate. Make the sauce for the shrimp/prawns. Start cooking the chicken and set the rice to boil. Finish cooking the shrimp/prawns and set out the ingredients for the Banana dessert.

Shrimp/prawns Tourkolimano (Greek style)

For the sauce:
4/3 tbsp finely chopped onion
4/3 tbsp olive oil
2 cloves garlic, crushed
1 cup/9 oz/250 g canned tomatoes, drained
salt
pepper

11 oz/300 g raw shrimp/prawns (fresh or frozen)
3/2 tbsp olive oil
2 tbsp/1 oz/25 g butter
2 tbsp brandy
2 tbsp Ouzo, anisette or Pernod
3 oz/80 g Feta (Greek cheese)

Prepare the sauce first: sauté the onion in the oil with the garlic cloves; discard the garlic when the onion turns golden brown; add the tomatoes, salt and pepper and cook until the sauce

has reduced and thickened. Meanwhile, fry the shrimp/prawns for 2-3 minutes in the oil and butter; pour in the brandy and Ouzo, heat and flame. Transfer the shrimp/prawns to a small ovenproof dish and cover with the sauce and thin slices of Feta cheese. Place in a preheated oven at 450°F/230°C/m 8 for 5 minutes or until the surface is lightly browned. Serve at once.

Preparation: 30 minutes.

Cantonese fried chicken

2 2-lb/900-g oven-ready chickens
1 clove garlic
salt
pepper
2 tbsp soy sauce
1 tbsp oil
2 tbsp flour
1 tsp ground ginger
oil for frying
1 tbsp cornstarch/cornflour
1/2 cup/4 fl oz/125 ml chicken stock
3/2 tbsp sherry
2 tbsp chopped scallion/spring onion
4 portions plain boiled rice

Rub the chicken portions with a cut clove of garlic and season with salt and pepper. Mix the soy sauce with 1 tbsp oil and pour over the chicken pieces in a bowl; leave to marinate for 5 minutes. Coat the chicken pieces lightly with a mixture of the flour and ground ginger. Deep fry the chicken until cooked through and golden brown on the outside. Place the fried chicken pieces in a heavy-bottomed saucepan; mix the cornstarch/cornflour with the stock and pour over the chicken. Add the sherry, cover tightly and simmer for 25 minutes. Arrange the chicken

pieces in a heated serving dish and garnish with chopped scallion/spring onion. Serve with boiled rice.

Preparation: 15 minutes.
Total time: 55 minutes.

Banana dessert
(can be cooked at the table)

4 ripe bananas
3 tbsp/1 1/2 oz/40 g butter
1/4 cup/2 oz/50 g sugar
1/2 tsp ground cinnamon
3/2 tbsp banana cream liqueur or maraschino
4/3 tbsp rum
4 portions vanilla ice cream

Peel the bananas and slice lengthwise in half. Heat the butter, sugar and ground cinnamon together in a large frying pan until the sugar has dissolved. Add the bananas and fry gently until they have started to soften. Pour in the liqueur and rum; heat gently and flame. Spoon the flaming spirit over the bananas with a long-handled spoon. Place two halved bananas on top of each portion of ice cream and pour over the remaining liqueur.

Preparation: 5 minutes.

MENU 83

Risotto with Barolo wine
Stuffed chicken breasts
Artichoke hearts with butter
Hovdessert
(ice cream with meringues and hot chocolate sauce)

Shopping list

14 oz/400 g chicken breasts ● 14 oz/400 g risotto rice ● 3 oz/80 g prosciutto/raw ham, machine sliced ● 2 oz/50 g freshly grated Parmesan cheese ● 4 oz/125 g Fontina or processed cheese slices ● 1 can artichoke hearts ● 4 oz/125 g plain chocolate ● 4 oz/125 g small meringues ● 12 oz/350 g vanilla ice cream.

From the store cupboard ● butter – milk – onion – Barolo wine – stock – Marsala – meat essence/extract – sugar – salt – pepper.

Work schedule ● Prepare the Stuffed chicken breasts. Start cooking the risotto. Gently heat

the artichoke hearts in butter. Finish the Stuffed chicken breasts. Make the chocolate sauce and keep hot.

Risotto with Barolo wine

1 tbsp finely chopped onion
6 tbsp/3 oz/80 g butter
2 cups/14 oz/400 g risotto rice
1 large glass Barolo wine
4 1/4 cups/1 3/4 pints/1 liter full-flavoured stock
1/4 cup/2 oz/50 g freshly grated Parmesan cheese

bat until they are very thin. Wrap the cheese in the prosciutto/raw ham and roll up inside a chicken breast. Secure with a cocktail stick. Season the stuffed rolls with salt and plenty of freshly ground pepper. Fry in butter until golden brown: turn down the heat, cover and cook very gently for 5 minutes. Add the Marsala and boil fast to reduce by half; pour in the diluted meat essence/extract and boil for a further minute. Remove the cocktail sticks and transfer the stuffed chicken breasts to a heated serving dish.

Preparation: 20 minutes.

Hovdessert (ice cream with meringues and hot chocolate sauce)

2 cups/12 oz/350 g vanilla ice cream
4 oz/125 g small meringues
4 oz/125 g plain chocolate
1 tbsp/1/2 oz/15 g butter
2 tbsp milk

Place the ice cream in individual glass dishes and top with the meringues. Melt the chocolate and butter in a basin over hot water, then stir in the milk. Serve the hot chocolate sauce separately.

Preparation: 5 minutes.

Fry the chopped onion gently in 2 tbsp/1 oz/25 g butter in a large risotto or paella pan. Add the rice and cook for 30 seconds. Pour in two-thirds of the wine and allow to evaporate completely. Pour in half the boiling stock, stir well and cook for about 18 minutes, adding more boiling stock (a ladleful at a time) when the rice has absorbed most of the liquid. After 15 minutes, add the remaining wine. Remove the risotto from the heat when still fairly moist. Add the remaining butter in pieces and the grated Parmesan cheese and mix well with a wooden spoon. Serve more grated Parmesan cheese separately.

Preparation: 30 minutes.

Stuffed chicken breasts

4 oz/125 g Fontina or processed cheese slices
14 oz/400 g chicken breasts
3 oz/80 g prosciutto/raw ham, machine sliced
salt
pepper
3 tbsp/1 1/2 oz/40 g butter
6/4 tbsp Marsala
1 tsp meat essence/extract, dissolved in 6/4 tbsp hot water

Cut the cheese into matchstick strips, as illustrated. Pound the chicken breasts with a meat

MENU 84

Oysters poached in Champagne
Sukiyaki
Oranges steeped in liqueur

Shopping list

24 oysters ● 1 lb/450 g tenderloin/fillet of beef, sliced wafer-thin ● 7 eggs ● 1 small carton light/single cream ● 1 small canned black truffle (optional) ● 9 oz/250 g rice, preferably Japanese (medium or short grain) ● 20 scallions/spring onions ● 11 oz/300 g watercress or fresh spinach ● 2 large heads celery ● 9 oz/250 g button mushrooms ● 1 can Japanese pickled vegetables (optional) ● 5 large oranges ● 1 small bottle soybean oil ● 1 bottle saké (Japanese rice wine) or dry white wine ● ½ bottle Champagne or sparkling dry white wine.

From the store cupboard ● butter – sugar – ground ginger – soy sauce – stock – Cointreau or Grand Marnier – monosodium glutamate (optional).

Work schedule ● Prepare the ingredients for the Sukiyaki. Peel the oranges and cut into small pieces; mix with the orange liqueur and sugar and place in the refrigerator to chill. Start cooking the oysters.

Oysters poached in Champagne

6/4 tbsp Champagne or sparkling dry white wine
24 oysters
3 egg yolks
¾ cup/4 fl oz/125 ml light/single cream
1 small canned black truffle (optional)
1½ tbsp/scant 1 oz/20 g butter

Open the shells with an oyster knife, remove the meat and reserve the liquor. Warm the oyster shells in the oven. Boil the Champagne in a small saucepan until reduced to half its original volume; remove from the heat and allow to cool. Add the oysters and 4/3 tbsp of their liquor. Return to the heat and warm the oysters

without boiling; drain and place in their shells. Beat the egg yolks lightly with the cream and warm over a low heat until the sauce thickens. Do not boil. Pour a little sauce over each oyster and decorate with slivers of black truffle warmed in butter.

Preparation: 25 minutes.

Sukiyaki

Sukiyaki is cooked at the table and calls for special utensils: a small spirit lamp, a wide straight-sided pan, chopsticks and small porcelain bowls.

Before each guest place the following:
   a small bowl for the boiled rice
   a small bowl containing lightly beaten egg
   a pair of chopsticks
In the center of the table you will need:
   a spirit lamp and straight-sided pan
   a platter of raw meat
   a platter of vegetables, cut into strips
   5 small bowls containing the ingredients to be
   added during cooking

On the meat platter
1 lb/450 g tenderloin/fillet of beef, sliced wafer-thin and cut into strips 1 in/2.5 cm wide

On the vegetable platter
20 scallions/spring onions, cut into strips
11 oz/300 g watercress or spinach, cut into strips
2 celery hearts, cut into thin strips
2-2½ cups/9 oz/250 g button mushrooms, thinly sliced
1 can Japanese pickled vegetables, well drained (optional)

In the small bowls

1. *3/2 tbsp soybean oil*
2. *2 tbsp saké or dry white wine*
3. *1 cup/9 fl oz/250 ml stock*
4. *4/3 tbsp soy sauce*
5. *a mixture of the following ingredients:*
   ½ tsp monosodium glutamate (optional)
   ½ tsp ground ginger
   2 tbsp superfine/caster sugar
   ½ tsp salt

Pour the oil into the straight-sided pan, heat over a high flame and brown the beef very quickly. Push the meat to one side and add the contents of the other 4 bowls at once. Add the vegetables in the following order, keeping them separate from each other whilst cooking: celery, scallions/spring onions, mushrooms and the Japanese pickled vegetables. Cook for 3 minutes, then add the watercress or spinach and cook for a further minute. The guests serve themselves directly from the pan, using their chopsticks and dipping the food in the raw beaten egg. Serve with plain boiled rice (1¼ cups/9 oz/250 g to serve 4).

Preparation before cooking at table: 30 minutes.

MENU 85

Cream of leek soup
Steak in beer
Sautéed potatoes
Baked bananas

Shopping list

4 9-oz/250-g top loin/entrecôte steaks ● 1 7-oz/200-g can cooked sliced button mushrooms ● 1 can cream of leek soup (4 servings) ● 14 fl oz/400 ml light/single cream ● 1 lb/450 g potatoes ● small bunch parsley ● 2 oz/50 g macaroons ● 4 bananas ● 1 small bottle of beer.

From the store cupboard ● butter – garlic – Worcestershire sauce – meat essence/extract – beer – sugar – rum – Cointreau – clarified butter (see p. 11) – salt – pepper.

Work schedule ● Set the potatoes to boil. Prepare the bananas for baking. Start cooking the Steak in beer. Place the bananas in the oven and heat the soup. Fry the potatoes in butter.

Cream of leek soup

The flavour and consistency of canned leek soup is greatly enhanced by the addition of ¾ cup/4 fl oz/125 ml light/single cream. Add to the soup while it is heating, but do not allow to boil.

Worcestershire sauce, mushrooms and diluted meat essence/extract; boil for 5 minutes and pour over the steaks.

Preparation: 15 minutes.

Baked bananas

4 bananas
3 tbsp/1½ oz/40 g butter
3/2 tbsp sugar
⅓ cup/3 fl oz/80 ml Cointreau
¼ cup/2 fl oz/60 ml rum
1½ cups/9 fl oz/250 ml light/single cream
4 macaroons, crumbled

Peel the bananas and slice lengthwise in half. Melt the butter in an oval ovenproof dish and arrange the bananas close to one another in a single layer. Sprinkle with sugar and bake in a preheated oven at 350°F/180°C/mk 4 for 8-10 minutes. Pour over the Cointreau and the rum, then add the cream, spooning it over the bananas and liqueur; sprinkle the surface with crumbled macaroons. Bake in the oven for a further 7-8 minutes, or until the top is lightly browned.

Preparation: 5 minutes.
Total time: 20 minutes.

Steak in beer

4 9-oz/250-g top loin/entrecôte steaks
1 clove garlic
salt
pepper
2 tbsp clarified butter
1 cup/8 fl oz/225 ml beer
4/3 tbsp Worcestershire sauce
1 7-oz/200-g can cooked sliced button mushrooms
½ tsp meat essence/extract dissolved in ¼ cup/2 fl oz/60 ml boiling water

Rub the steaks with the cut clove of garlic, season with salt and pepper and brown on both sides in the very hot clarified butter. Lower the heat and cook according to preference (rare, medium rare, etc.). Remove the steaks, drain and keep warm between two hot plates. Add the beer to the juices and butter in the pan and boil until the liquid has reduced by half. Add the

MENU 86

Goose liver pâté in puff pastry
Champagne chicken
Boiled rice
Glazed onions
Pears flamed in brandy

Shopping list

1 7-oz/200-g can pâté de foie gras truffé (goose liver pâté with truffles) ● 1 large can pears ● 1 jar apricot jam ● 1 3-lb/1.4-kg oven-ready chicken ● 18 fl oz/500 ml Champagne ● 9 oz/250 g rice ● 4 oz/125 g puff or flaky pastry (homemade or frozen) ● 3 eggs ● 9 fl oz/250 ml light/single cream ● 1½ lb/700 g small onions or shallots.

From the store cupboard ● butter – onion – shallot – flour – sugar – Cognac – salt – pepper.

Work schedule ● Start cooking the chicken. Cut out and cook the puff pastry for the goose liver slices. Cook the onions and boil the rice. Warm the pears in their own juice and spread the goose liver pâté on the pastry.

Goose liver pâté in puff pastry

4 oz/125 g puff or flaky pastry (homemade or frozen)
1 7-oz/200-g can pâté de foie gras truffé (goose liver pâté with truffles)
1 egg

Roll out the pastry 1 in/2.5 cm thick and use a fluted pastry wheel to cut out pear shapes 4-5 in/10-12 cm long. Place on a lightly dampened baking sheet, prick the pastry with a fork and brush lightly with beaten egg. Place in a preheated oven at 350°F/180°C/mk 4 for 10-12 minutes or until well risen and golden brown. Cut open the top of each pastry layer. Just before serving, reheat the pastry cases in the oven for a minute; spread goose liver pâté liberally on the bottom half and sandwich together with the browned top half.

Preparation: 8 minutes.
Total time: 20 minutes.

Champagne chicken

3 tbsp/1½ oz/40 g butter
2 tbsp finely chopped onion
1 tbsp finely chopped shallot
1 3-lb/1.4-kg oven-ready chicken, cut into 8 portions
salt
pepper
2¼ cups/18 fl oz/500 ml Champagne
1 tbsp/½ oz/15 g butter
1 level tbsp flour
1½ cups/9 fl oz/250 ml light/single cream
2 egg yolks
1¼ cups/9 oz/250 g rice (uncooked weight), boiled

Place 3 tbsp/1½ oz/40 g butter, chopped onion, shallot and jointed chicken in a heavy-bottomed saucepan and season with salt and pepper. Cover tightly and cook over a low heat for 20 minutes, turning frequently to prevent the chicken pieces from burning. Pour in the Champagne and bring to a fast boil; lower the heat and cover. While the chicken is simmering in the Champagne, melt 1 tbsp/½ oz/15 g butter in a small saucepan, stir in the flour and cook for 30 seconds. Remove from the heat, allow to cool slightly and add a little of the cooking liquid from the chicken. Bring to the boil, stirring constantly, and add to the saucepan containing the chicken and Champagne. When the chicken is cooked, remove from the pan, drain and keep warm. Add half the cream to the cooking liquid and boil rapidly until reduced. Skim off excess fat and turn down the heat; stir in the remaining cream mixed with the two egg yolks and heat until the sauce thickens slightly. Do not allow to boil. When the rice is tender but still firm, drain and rinse with boiling water to keep the grains separate. Arrange the rice in a ring on a heated serving platter; place the chicken pieces in the center and cover with the sauce just before serving.

Preparation: 15 minutes.
Total time: 1 hour.

Glazed onions

2 tbsp/1 oz/25 g butter
1½ lb/700 g small onions or shallots, trimmed and peeled
salt
pepper

Melt the butter in a frying pan and add the

133

onions; sauté gently until they begin to colour and then add salt, pepper and 2-3 tbsp boiling water. Cover the pan tightly and cook slowly, turning the onions gently every now and then and adding a little more boiling water when necessary. The onions should simmer rather than fry.

Preparation: 5 minutes.
Total time: about 30 minutes.

Pears flamed in brandy

8 canned pear halves
2 tbsp apricot jam

½ cup/2½ oz/70 g sugar
6/4 tbsp Cognac

Heat the pears gently in the juice from the can; remove from the liquid with a slotted spoon and place on a very hot serving dish. Heat the apricot jam with 2-3 tbsp of the reserved pear juice and boil briefly. Pour the glaze through a sieve over the pears and sprinkle with the sugar. Heat the Cognac, set it alight and pour the flaming spirit over the pears. Serve immediately.

Preparation: 10 minutes.

MENU 87

Tyrolean Speck
Cream of artichoke soup
Broiled/grilled pigeons
Duchesse tomatoes
Strawberry mousse

Shopping list

4 pigeons ● 11 oz/300 g Tyrolean Speck (cured, smoked pork fat, rolled in paprika: eat raw spread on wholemeal or black bread) ● 8 slices smoked bacon (preferably streaky) ● 1 large can cream of artichoke soup (4 servings) ● 12 oz/350 g frozen strawberries ● 3 eggs ● 1 small carton single/light cream ● 1 small carton whipping cream ● rosemary ● 4 large or 8 small ripe tomatoes ● ½ lb/225 g potatoes ● 1 sachet/½ oz/15 g powdered gelatine ● 7 oz/200 g vanilla ice cream.

From the store cupboard ● butter – oil – nutmeg – maraschino – sugar – salt – pepper.

Work schedule ● Set the potatoes to boil for the Duchesse tomatoes and start the Strawberry mousse. Prepare the pigeons for broiling/grilling and cut the tomatoes as directed; place in the oven with their potato filling and start broiling/grilling the pigeons. Heat the Cream of artichoke soup.

Cream of artichoke soup

Heat the soup according to the manufacturer's instructions. Stir in light/single cream, allowing 2 tbsp per serving. Once the cream has been added, do not allow the soup to boil.

Broiled/grilled pigeons

4 pigeons
salt
pepper
1 tbsp oil
1 small bunch rosemary
¼ cup/2 oz/50 g melted butter
8 slices smoked bacon (preferably streaky)

Split the pigeons lengthwise in half, season with

salt and pepper and brush lightly with oil. Start to broil/grill the birds; when they are half-cooked, dip the bunch of rosemary in the melted butter and use to baste the pigeons. Repeat at frequent intervals until all the butter is used. Broil/grill the bacon and serve as a garnish.

Preparation: 40 minutes.

Duchesse tomatoes

½ lb/225 g potatoes
2 egg yolks
1 whole egg
4 large or 8 small ripe tomatoes
1½ tbsp/scant 1 oz/20 g butter
salt
pepper
nutmeg

Prepare a Duchesse potato mixture (see p. 82), adding the 2 egg yolks and half the lightly beaten whole egg to the creamed potatoes. If large tomatoes are used, slice in half; if small, cut a section off the top of each. Scoop out the seeds, sprinkle inside with salt and turn upside down to drain. Spoon the Duchesse potato mixture into an icing bag and pipe the potato into the tomatoes. Brush with the remaining beaten egg and bake in a preheated oven at 350°F/180°C/mk 4 until the potato is golden brown.

Preparation: 55 minutes.

Strawberry mousse

2 cups/12 oz/350 g frozen strawberries
½ cup/4 fl oz/125 ml maraschino
1 cup/7 oz/200 g vanilla ice cream
1 sachet/½ oz/15 g powdered gelatine
5/3 tbsp sugar syrup (boil equal quantities of sugar and water together until the sugar has totally dissolved)
4/3 tbsp sweetened whipped cream

Place half the strawberries in a blender with the maraschino and liquidize; add the ice cream in two or three lots, blending after each addition. Soften the gelatine in a little cold water and melt gently (do not allow to boil) in the hot sugar syrup. Blend into the liquidized mixture. Distribute the remaining strawberries between four glass dishes, reserving four for decoration. Pour the blended mixture over the whole strawberries and chill in the coldest part of the refrigerator. Just before serving, top with sweetened whipped cream and a whole strawberry.

Preparation: 15 minutes.
Total time: 1 hour.

MENU 88

Chicken Maryland salad
Liver and bacon with bacon-flavoured sautéed potatoes
Rainbow sundae

Shopping list

12 oz/350 g cooked or raw chicken or turkey breasts ● 1 lb/450 g calf's liver ● 1 bottle Melba sauce ● 1 14-oz/400-g can sweetcorn ● 1 can peppers, preferably yellow and red ● 8 thin slices smoked streaky bacon ● 1 medium-sized can peach halves ● 1 egg ● 1 lemon ● 1 small carton whipping cream ● 1 lb/450 g potatoes ● small bunch parsley ● 5 oz/150 g vanilla ice cream ● 5 oz/50 g pistachio ice cream ● 2 oz/50 g hundreds-and-thousands ● 2 oz/50 g ice cream wafers or finger biscuits (langues de chat).

From the store cupboard ● butter – onion – olive oil – sunflower oil – sugar – salt – pepper.

Work schedule ● If raw chicken breasts are used, cook in the pressure cooker or poach. Set the potatoes to boil. Hard-boil the egg and prepare the chicken salad. Assemble the ingredients for the dessert. Cook the liver and bacon and finish the potatoes.

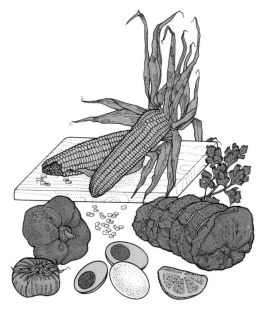

1 tbsp sunflower oil
salt
8 thin slices smoked streaky bacon
a little butter
1 lb/450 g boiled potatoes

Slice the liver to the desired thickness and brush both sides with oil. Broil/grill briefly and transfer immediately to a heated serving dish. Sprinkle lightly with salt and keep warm. Place the bacon slices in a single layer in a large frying pan without fat or oil and fry over a moderate heat until the fat has become translucent. Place the bacon slices on top of the cooked liver. Add a little butter to the bacon fat in the pan. Add the boiled, sliced potatoes and fry until golden brown on both sides.

Preparation: 15 minutes.

Chicken Maryland salad

12 oz/350 g chicken or turkey breasts
1 14-oz/400-g can sweetcorn
1 can peppers, preferably yellow and red
1 tbsp chopped onion
1 tbsp chopped parsley
3/2 tbsp olive oil
juice of 1/2 lemon
salt
pepper
1 hard-boiled egg, cut lengthwise into quarters
small bunch parsley

Dice the chicken and place in a bowl with the well-drained sweetcorn, the finely diced peppers, the chopped onion and parsley; mix and dress with oil, lemon juice, salt and pepper. Transfer to a deep serving dish and garnish with the hard-boiled egg and sprigs of parsley.

Preparation: 15 minutes.

Liver and bacon with bacon-flavoured sautéed potatoes

1 lb/450 g calf's liver

Rainbow sundae

scant 1 cup/5 oz/150 g vanilla ice cream
2 canned peach halves, drained and diced
1/2 cup/3 1/2 fl oz/100 ml Melba sauce
scant 1 cup/5 oz/150 g pistachio ice cream
6/4 tbsp sweetened whipped cream
1 tbsp hundreds-and-thousands
4 ice cream wafers or finger biscuits

Place the vanilla ice cream in individual sundae dishes; add the diced peaches and cover with Melba sauce. Add the pistachio ice cream and top with sweetened whipped cream. Decorate with hundreds-and-thousands and a wafer or finger biscuit.

Preparation: 10 minutes.

MENU 89

**George's spaghetti
Turkey breasts Hungarian style
Peppers in sweet and sour sauce
Strawberries with Grand Marnier**

Shopping list

1 1/4 lb/600 g turkey breast, cut crosswise into scallops/escalopes ● 1 7-oz/200-g can sliced button mushrooms ● 2 oz/50 g freshly grated Parmesan cheese ● 2 3/4 oz/75 g prosciutto/raw ham, machine sliced ● 14 oz/400 g very thin spaghetti ● 1 packet dried mushrooms (Italian *porcini* or French *cèpes*) ● 4 large ripe tomatoes or 1 14-oz/400-g can tomatoes ● small bunch parsley ● 1 lemon ● 1 orange ● 3 large peppers, preferably yellow, red and green ● 1 small carton sour cream ● 11 oz/300 g fresh or frozen strawberries ● 1 small carton whipping cream.

From the store cupboard ● butter – onion – paprika – brandy – flour – sunflower oil – sugar – wine vinegar – dry white wine – Grand Marnier – salt – pepper.

Work schedule • Soak the dried mushrooms in warm water for 15 minutes. Prepare the strawberries and leave to marinate in the refrigerator. Cook the sweet and sour peppers and make the sauce for the spaghetti. Set the water to boil for the spaghetti and cook the turkey breasts.

George's spaghetti

scant 1 oz/20 g dried mushrooms
3 tbsp/1½ oz/40 g butter
2 tbsp finely chopped onion
2¾ oz/75 g prosciutto/raw ham, machine sliced
4 large ripe tomatoes or 1 14-oz/400-g can tomatoes, drained and seeds removed
salt
pepper
14 oz/400 g very thin spaghetti
4/3 tbsp freshly grated Parmesan cheese
2 tbsp finely chopped parsley

Soak the dried mushrooms for 15 minutes in warm water until soft and plumped up; drain and chop. Heat half the butter in a large frying pan and sauté the chopped onion over a low heat. Add the prosciutto/raw ham, cut into strips, and the mushrooms and cook for 2 minutes. Add the chopped tomatoes, season with salt and pepper and simmer for a further 10 minutes. Drain the spaghetti when it is tender but still firm and add to the frying pan with the sauce. Add the remaining butter cut into small pieces and the Parmesan cheese. Sprinkle with the chopped parsley and transfer immediately to a heated serving dish.

Preparation: 25 minutes.

Turkey breasts Hungarian style

1¼ lb/600 g turkey breast, cut crosswise into scallops/escalopes
salt
pepper
2 tbsp flour
¼ cup/2 oz/50 g butter
1 tsp paprika
1 tbsp brandy
1 7-oz/200-g can sliced button mushrooms
1 cup/5 fl oz/150 ml sour cream
¼ tbsp lemon juice

Pound the turkey scallops/escalopes with a meat bat; season with salt and pepper, coat lightly with flour and fry gently in butter. Remove from the pan, drain and keep warm between two hot plates. Add the paprika to the juices in the pan; cook gently for 30 seconds then add the brandy, mushrooms, sour cream and lemon juice. Boil for 1 minute, lower the heat and return the turkey pieces to the sauce for a few seconds before serving.

Preparation: 15 minutes.

Peppers in sweet and sour sauce

3 large peppers, preferably 1 yellow, 1 red and 1 green
4/3 tbsp oil
1 rounded tbsp sugar
¼ cup/2½ fl oz/75 ml dry white wine
salt
2 tbsp wine vinegar

Remove the stalk, seeds and membrane from inside the peppers and cut into ½-in/1-cm strips. Heat the oil in a high-sided frying pan; add the

peppers and sugar, cover and cook over a very high heat, shaking frequently, until the peppers have started to dry out and are fairly tender. Pour in the wine and continue to cook over a high heat. When the peppers are tender, add the salt and vinegar and cook for a further 30 seconds. Prepared in this way, peppers are equally good hot or lukewarm.

Preparation: 15 minutes.
Total time: 25 minutes.

Strawberries with Grand Marnier

2¼ cups/11 oz/300 g fresh or frozen strawberries
4/3 tbsp sugar
½ cup/4 fl oz/125 ml sweetened whipped cream

4/3 tbsp Grand Marnier
1 tbsp fresh orange juice
½ tsp finely grated orange peel

Place all the ingredients except for the whipped cream (which will be used for decoration) in a large bowl and mix gently. Leave to chill in the refrigerator. Just before serving, spoon the strawberries and the juice into individual dishes or a large crystal bowl and top with whipped cream.

Preparation: 10 minutes.
Refrigeration: 50 minutes.

MENU 90

Prosciutto and bresaola
(raw ham and Italian dried salt beef)
Bisque d'écrevisses (crayfish soup)
Veal cutlets/escalopes with Calvados
Buttered spinach
Chocolate eclairs

Shopping list

7 oz/200 g prosciutto/raw ham, very thinly sliced • 5 oz/150 g bresaola (dried salt beef), very thinly sliced • 14 oz/400 g veal cutlets/escalopes • 1 can crayfish soup (4 servings) • 1 small carton light/single cream • 1 large cooking apple • 1 lemon • 1 lb/450 g frozen spinach • chocolate eclairs.

From the store cupboard • butter – Calvados – salt – pepper.

Work schedule • While the crayfish soup is heating, cook the spinach. Drain the spinach well and toss in butter. Start cooking the veal cutlets/escalopes.

Bisque d'écrevisses
(crayfish soup)

Heat the canned crayfish soup and stir in 1-2 tbsp light/single cream. This will improve the flavour and texture of the soup considerably. Do not allow the soup to boil.

Veal cutlets/escalopes with Calvados
(can be cooked at the table)

14 oz/400 g veal cutlets/escalopes
3 tbsp/1½ oz/40 g butter
a little fresh lemon juice
1 large cooking apple, shaped into balls with a melon baller
salt
pepper
3/2 tbsp Calvados
4/3 tbsp light/single cream

Pound the cutlets/escalopes between sheets of waxed paper until they are very thin. Heat the butter in a frying pan, add the cutlets/escalopes and fry briskly. Add a few drops of lemon juice and turn the meat. Add the apple balls and stir. Lower the heat to finish cooking the veal; season lightly with salt and pepper. Add the Calvados, heat and then flame, shaking the pan gently. Pour in the cream and heat almost to boiling point; cover and remove from the heat.

Preparation: 10 minutes.

MENU 91

**Rossolnick
(Russian cucumber soup)
Roast chicken with tarragon**
Pommes de terre noisette
Coffee gâteau

Shopping list

1 3-lb/1.3-kg oven-ready chicken ● 3¼ lb/1½ kg cucumbers ● 2 carrots ● 2 turnips ● 1 head celery ● 1 lemon ● 2¼ lb/1 kg new potatoes ● 1 large bunch fresh tarragon or 1 tsp dried ● ½ pint/300 ml light/single cream ● 4 eggs ● 2 oz/50 g gherkins ● 1 coffee gâteau.

From the store cupboard ● chicken stock – butter – salt – pepper.

Work schedule ● Place the chicken in the oven to roast. Liquidize the cucumbers and start cooking the soup. Place the Pommes de terre noisette in the oven (see p. 21).

Rossolnick
(Russian cucumber soup)

2¼ cups/18 fl oz/500 ml chicken stock
3 cups/1¼ pints/750 ml cucumber juice (made by liquidizing the cucumbers)
2 carrots, thinly sliced
2 gherkins, thinly sliced
2 small turnips, thinly sliced
1 stick celery, thinly sliced
2 egg yolks
1½ cups/9 fl oz/250 ml light/single cream

Place the stock in a large saucepan with two-thirds of the liquidized cucumbers, the carrots, gherkins, turnips and celery and boil gently for 40 minutes. Remove from the heat, add the remaining cucumber juice and the two egg yolks mixed with the cream. Return to the heat and bring almost to boiling point.

Preparation: 5 minutes.
Total time: 50 minutes.

Roast chicken with tarragon

1 3-lb/1.3-kg oven-ready chicken
1 lemon
1 large bunch fresh tarragon or 1 tsp dried
6 tbsp/3 oz/80 g butter
salt
pepper
2 egg yolks
3/2 tbsp light/single cream

Wash the chicken, dry with paper towels and rub inside and out with the freshly cut surface of ½ lemon. Mix the tarragon with half the butter and place inside the chicken, with a little salt and some freshly ground pepper. Truss the chicken

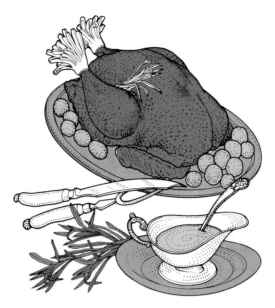

firmly; sprinkle with salt and pepper, brush with the remaining melted butter and place in a roasting pan. Roast in a preheated oven at 400°F/200°C/mk 6 until the juices run clear when a skewer is inserted deep into the thigh. Remove the chicken from the oven and place on a heated serving platter. Place the roasting pan over low heat, add 1 tbsp water and stir with a wooden spoon. Stir in the egg yolks mixed with the cream and as soon as the sauce begins to thicken pour into a heated sauceboat.

Preparation: 5 minutes.
Total time: 1 hour.

MENU 92

Mussels Dieppe style
Quails with cream
Peas with butter
Mixed salad
Fresh fruit

Shopping list

8 quails ● 2¼ lb/1 kg mussels ● 1 packet frozen peas or 2¼ lb/1 kg fresh peas ● 9 fl oz/250 ml milk ● 18 fl oz/500 ml light/single cream ● small bunch parsley ● fresh sage leaves ● rosemary ● 1 stick celery ● 1 carrot ● fresh fruit ● mixed salad ingredients.

From the store cupboard ● butter – flour – nutmeg – cayenne pepper – garlic – onion – dry white wine – olive oil – wine vinegar – sugar – lemon – salt – pepper.

Work schedule ● Make the béchamel sauce. Prepare the quails for cooking. Start preparing the mussels. Cook the quails and prepare the peas. Wash and dry the salad.

Mussels Dieppe style

2¼ lb/1 kg mussels
1 cup/9 fl oz/250 ml béchamel sauce
1 cup/6 fl oz/175 ml light/single cream
cayenne pepper
finely chopped parsley

Scrub the mussels under cold running water and discard any that are open. Place in a large frying pan over low heat. When the shells open remove the meat, reserving one half of each shell, and pour any liquid back into the pan. Boil the liquid from the mussels until it is reduced by half and use to make the béchamel sauce. Heat the béchamel sauce with the cream over moderate heat; bring almost to the boil and add a pinch of cayenne pepper. Place the shells in the oven to warm: arrange on a heated serving dish, fill each shell with 1 or 2 mussels and cover with the sauce. Sprinkle with chopped parsley.

Preparation: 5 minutes.
Total time: 30 minutes.

Quails with cream

8 quails
salt
pepper
2 tbsp flour
¼ cup/2 oz/50 g butter
a finely chopped mixture of:
    2 fresh sage leaves
    ½ tsp rosemary leaves
    1 clove garlic
    1 small onion
    ½ stick celery
    1 small carrot
⅔ cup/5 fl oz/150 ml dry white wine
scant ¾ cup/4 fl oz/125 ml light/single cream

Season the quails with salt and pepper and coat lightly with flour. Melt the butter in a large, heavy-bottomed saucepan. Place the quails in the pan and cover tightly. Fry gently over a moderate heat, turning from time to time and replacing the lid immediately. When the quails are tender, add the finely chopped mixture of herbs, garlic and vegetables and fry gently. Pour in the white wine and cook until it has evaporated. Add the cream and heat almost to boiling point. Remove the quails and arrange on a heated serving platter; strain the sauce through a sieve over the quails and serve immediately.

Preparation: 15 minutes.
Total time: 35 minutes.

MENU 93

Cream of turtle soup
Chicken legs with goose liver pâté
Buttered carrots and Brussels sprouts
Ice cream sundae with chocolate sauce

Shopping list

4 chicken legs, boned ● 1 can turtle soup (2 servings) ● 1 can consommé (2 servings) ● 1 4-oz/125-g can pâté de foie gras ● 4 eggs ● 14 fl oz/400 ml heavy/double cream ● 7 fl oz/200 ml light/single cream ● 4 oz/120 g rice ● 2 oz/50 g pine nuts ● 12 oz/350 g vanilla ice cream ● 4 oz/125 g plain chocolate ● 2 oz/50 g chocolate hundreds-and-thousands ● ice cream wafers or finger biscuits (langues de chat) ● 1 lb/450 g Brussels sprouts ● 1 large can cooked baby carrots.

From the store cupboard ● butter – cayenne pepper – onion – stock – flour – dry white wine – superfine/caster sugar – milk – salt – pepper.

Work schedule ● Prepare the chicken legs and start cooking the rice. Steam the Brussels sprouts. Start cooking the stuffed chicken legs and toss the Brussels sprouts and carrots in butter. Make the soup and prepare the chocolate sauce (see p. 129) for the Ice cream sundae.

Cream of turtle soup

⅔ cup/4 fl oz/125 ml heavy/double cream
3 egg yolks
1 can turtle soup (2 servings)
1 can consommé (2 servings)
½ tsp cayenne pepper

Whip the cream but do not sweeten. Place the egg yolks, turtle soup and consommé in the top half of a double boiler. Place the double boiler over a gentle heat and stir until the soup thickens slightly. Pour the soup into individual consommé cups; float whipped cream on top, sprinkle with cayenne pepper and place under a hot broiler/grill for a few seconds.

Preparation: 15 minutes.

Opposite:
Menu 88, page 135

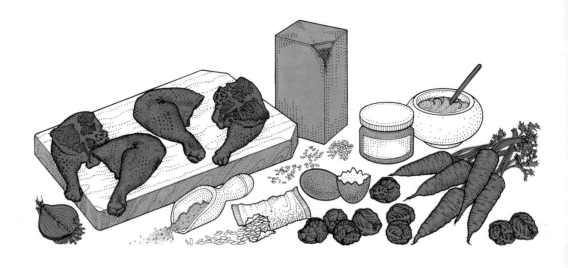

Chicken legs with goose liver pâté

½ cup/4 oz/125 g rice
1 egg yolk
1 4-oz/125-g can pâté de foie gras
2 tbsp pine nuts
4 chicken legs, boned
salt
pepper
flour
¼ cup/2 oz/50 g butter
½ onion, finely sliced
⅔ cup/5 fl oz/150 ml dry white wine
generous 1 cup/7 fl oz/200 ml light/single cream
scant 1 cup/7 fl oz/200 ml stock

Boil the rice for 9 minutes in salted water; drain and stir in the egg yolk and the pâté de foie gras; add the pine nuts, mix well and leave to cool. Pound the boned chicken legs between two sheets of greaseproof paper until very thin. Place equal amounts of the rice stuffing on each portion of chicken; roll up and secure with a cocktail stick. Season with salt and pepper, roll in flour and fry gently in butter. When the chicken is tender, add the finely sliced onion and fry gently. Pour in the wine and cook until it has evaporated. Pour in the cream and stock and boil until the sauce has thickened.

Preparation: 5 minutes.
Total time: 35 minutes.

Ice cream sundae with chocolate sauce

1½ cups/9 fl oz/250 ml heavy/double cream
2 tbsp superfine/caster sugar
2 cups/12 oz/350 g vanilla ice cream
chocolate sauce (see p. 129)
1 tbsp chocolate hundreds-and-thousands
ice cream wafers or finger biscuits (langues de chat)

Whip the cream, adding the sugar gradually as the cream begins to thicken. Place one or two scoops of ice cream in each sundae dish; cover with chocolate sauce and top with whipped cream. Decorate with chocolate hundreds-and-thousands and ice cream wafers or finger biscuits.

Preparation: 10 minutes.

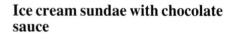

MENU 94

Lobster salad Tahiti
Spatchcock chickens
Buttered artichoke hearts
Pears with chocolate sauce

Opposite:
Menu 96, page 148

Shopping list

1 1½-lb/700-g cooked lobster ● 2 small coconuts ● 2 1½-lb/700-g spring chickens ● 2 heads celery ● 1 cos lettuce ● 1 bunch radishes ● 1 small apple ● 1 small cucumber ● 2 oz/50 g pitted black olives ● 2 oz/50 g pistachio nuts ● small bunch parsley ● 1 lemon ● 1 bunch watercress ● 1 can pear halves ● 12 oz/350 g canned or frozen artichoke hearts ● 11 oz/300 g vanilla ice cream ● 4 oz/125 g plain chocolate ● 2 oz/50 g toasted flaked almonds ● 9 fl oz/250 ml whipping cream ● 1 small jar mayonnaise.

From the store cupboard ● butter – milk – tomato ketchup – Tabasco sauce – brandy – fresh breadcrumbs – salt – pepper.

Work schedule ● Place the sundae dishes in the refrigerator to chill. Prepare the Tahiti salad and chill in the refrigerator. Cook the chickens. Heat the artichoke hearts in butter. Make the chocolate sauce (see p.129) and prepare the Pears with chocolate sauce.

Lobster salad Tahiti

2 small coconuts
1 1½-lb/700-g cooked lobster
2 celery hearts, cut into thin strips
1 cos lettuce, roughly torn
1 small apple, diced
1 small cucumber, diced
½ cup/4 fl oz/125ml mayonnaise
1 tbsp tomato ketchup
a few drops Tabasco sauce

2 tbsp brandy
salt
To garnish:
a few radishes, cut into 'flowers'
a few black olives, pitted and halved
a few pistachio nuts, split in half

Split the coconuts in half and scrape out some of the flesh. Chop the coconut flesh finely and mix with all the other ingredients. Season to taste. Fill the shells with this mixture and garnish with a few radish 'flowers', black olives and pistachio nuts. Chill in the refrigerator for as long as possible before serving.

Preparation: 20 minutes.

Spatchcock chickens

2 1½-lb/700-g spring chickens
salt
pepper
¼ cup/2 oz/50 g butter
fresh breadcrumbs
6 tbsp/3 oz/80 g Maître d'hôtel butter (see p. 112)
watercress

Split the chickens down the breastbone and flatten with a heavy meat bat. Thread them on to two long skewers to keep them flat as they cook. Season with salt and pepper and fry in hot butter; turn down the heat a little when the

chickens begin to brown. Drain, then press fresh breadcrumbs firmly on to the side covered with skin. Place in a large shallow ovenproof dish and brown the top quickly under a hot broiler/grill; transfer to a heated serving platter and dot with small pieces of Maître d'hôtel butter. Garnish with plenty of fresh watercress.

Preparation: 55 minutes.

Pears with chocolate sauce

scant 2 cups/11 oz/300 g vanilla ice cream

4 canned pear halves
chocolate sauce (see p. 129)
1½ cups/9 fl oz/250 ml sweetened whipped cream
1 tbsp toasted flaked almonds

Place an equal quantity of ice cream in each of the well-chilled sundae dishes. Place a pear half on top and cover with chocolate sauce. Top with sweetened whipped cream and sprinkle with the toasted almonds.

Preparation: 10 minutes.

MENU 95

Avgolemono (Greek chicken and lemon soup)
Quick hamburgers
Potato croquettes
Mixed salad
Ice cream gâteau

Shopping list

1 boiling fowl ● 4 ready-made hamburgers or 1¼ lb/600 g ground/minced lean beef ● 3½ oz/100 g finely chopped veal suet ● 1 stick celery ● 1 carrot ● 1 onion ● bay leaf ● thyme ● small bunch parsley ● 2 lemons ● 1 lb/450 g potatoes ● mixed salad ingredients ● 4 eggs ● ½ white loaf of bread ● 9 fl oz/250 ml light/single cream ● 1 ice cream gâteau.

From the store cupboard ● butter – garlic – flour – nutmeg – breadcrumbs – sunflower oil – olive oil – mustard powder – Dijon mustard – tomato ketchup – salt – pepper.

Work schedule ● Make the chicken stock in the pressure cooker; boil the potatoes. Mix and shape the hamburgers (unless ready-made are used). Wash and drain the salad. Strain the chicken stock and make the soup. Mash the potatoes and make the croquettes. Cook the hamburgers and fry the potato croquettes.

Avgolemono (Greek chicken and lemon soup)

1 boiling fowl
1 small stick celery
½ carrot
¼ onion
1 clove garlic
salt
3 tbsp/1½ oz/40 g butter
¼ cup + 3 tbsp/1½ oz/40 g flour
4/3 tbsp lemon juice
bouquet garni: bay leaf, thyme and parsley tied together in a piece of muslin
2 egg yolks
1½ cups/9 fl oz/250 ml light/single cream
finely grated lemon peel
croûtons, dried and crisped in the oven

Cook the chicken for 45 minutes in a pressure cooker with the celery, carrot, onion, garlic, salt and just enough water to cover the bird. Skim any fat from the surface of the stock. Melt the butter in a tall, heavy-bottomed cooking pot; stir in the flour and cook briefly. Remove from the heat and allow to cool slightly. Stir in 2 ladles of strained chicken stock, return to the heat and bring gradually to the boil, stirring continuously. Add sufficient stock for 4 servings of soup; add the lemon juice and bouquet garni and boil for 15 minutes. Remove from the heat, discard the bouquet garni and stir in the 2 egg yolks mixed with the cream. Reheat the soup, stirring continuously, but do not allow to boil. Serve immediately. Hand round a small dish of finely grated lemon peel and croûtons for garnish.

Preparation: 1 hour.

Quick hamburgers

2½ cups/1¼ lb/600 g ground/minced lean beef
⅔ cup/3½ oz/100 g finely chopped veal suet
1 tbsp cold water
salt
pepper
½ tbsp oil
or
4 ready-made hamburgers

Mix the beef thoroughly with the veal suet, water, salt and pepper; shape into 4 large hamburgers 1¼ in/3 cm thick. Brush the hamburgers lightly on both sides with oil and cook on the griddle or in a frying pan, according to preference (rare, medium rare or well done). Serve with at least two types of mustard and tomato ketchup.

Preparation: 15 minutes.

Potato croquettes

1 lb/450 g potatoes
1 egg yolk
salt
pepper
nutmeg
oil for frying
flour
1 whole egg, beaten
breadcrumbs

Boil the potatoes in their skins in salted water; drain well and place in a hot oven for 2-3 minutes to dry out any remaining moisture. Peel and mash the potatoes, then beat in the egg yolk, salt, pepper and a little grated nutmeg. Mould into sausage shapes 2 in/5 cm long and ¾ in/2 cm in diameter. Heat the oil in an electric fryer to very hot. Coat the potato croquettes lightly with flour, dip in the remaining beaten egg, roll in breadcrumbs and deep fry until they are pale golden brown.

Preparation: 10 minutes.
Total time: 50 minutes.

Seafood starter
Poached salmon steaks
Green salad
Bread and butter pudding

Shopping list

4 4-oz/125-g fresh salmon steaks ● 1 jar seafood salad (baby octopus and squid) to serve 4 ● 1 egg ● 2 lemons ● small bunch parsley ● 1 tomato ● 1 large lettuce ● 1 tube mayonnaise ● 9 oz/250 g Russian salad ● small bunch radishes ● 4 artichokes (optional) ● 18 fl oz/500 ml milk ● ½ white loaf of bread ● 2 oz/50 g seedless white raisins/sultanas ● 2 oz/50 g chopped mixed peel.

From the store cupboard ● butter – white wine vinegar – peppercorns – onion – nutmeg – bay leaf – superfine/caster sugar – brandy or rum – salt.

Work schedule ● Poach the salmon steaks and leave to cool. Place the Bread and butter pudding in the oven; wash and drain the lettuce. Place the salmon steaks on a serving platter. Arrange the seafood starter on individual plates or shells on a bed of lettuce.

Poached salmon steaks

4 4-oz/125-g fresh salmon steaks
4¼ cups/1¾ pints/1 liter water
4/3 tbsp white wine vinegar
½ lemon, sliced
¼ onion, sliced
8 peppercorns
1 bay leaf

salt
small bunch parsley
a few radishes
4 lemon wedges
1 tomato, quartered
1 hard-boiled egg, quartered
9 oz/250 g Russian salad
4 artichoke cups (optional)
1 small tube mayonnaise

Place the salmon steaks in a fairly large saucepan. Cover with water, add the vinegar, sliced lemon, onion, peppercorns, bay leaf and plenty of salt. Bring to the boil; turn down the heat immediately and simmer gently for 7-8 minutes. Remove from the heat and leave to cool; remove the steaks carefully with a fish slice and place on a serving platter. Garnish with parsley, a few radishes, lemon wedges, pieces of tomato and hard-boiled egg. Serve with Russian salad in artichoke cups (optional). If time is no problem the salmon steaks may be glazed in aspic for a more special finishing touch. Serve the mayonnaise in a bowl or sauceboat.

Preparation: 1 hour.

Bread and butter pudding

6 slices of bread, crusts removed
½ cup/4 oz/125 g butter

¼ cup/2 oz/50 g superfine/caster sugar
2 tbsp seedless white raisins/sultanas, softened in
warm water
1 tbsp chopped mixed peel
2 tbsp brandy or rum
2 eggs
1¼ cups/½ pint/300 ml milk
finely grated peel of ½ lemon
pinch grated nutmeg

Spread the slices of bread generously with butter on both sides and cut each slice in half diagonally to form two triangles. Butter a 3-pint/2½-pint/1½-liter soufflé dish and arrange a layer of buttered slices to cover the bottom. Sprinkle with a little sugar, a few seedless white raisins/sultanas and a little chopped peel; continue layering the ingredients until all the bread has been used. Finish with a layer of bread (reserve a little of the sugar) and sprinkle the brandy (or rum) over the top. Beat the eggs in a bowl. Bring the milk and grated lemon peel to the boil, remove from the heat and pour slowly on to the eggs, beating vigorously. Pour the milk and egg mixture into the soufflé dish, trickling it down the sides rather than over the top. Sprinkle the surface of the pudding with the remaining sugar and a pinch of nutmeg. Bake in a preheated oven at 350°F/180°C/mk 4 for 40 minutes or until the pudding has risen slightly and the top is golden brown. Serve hot or warm straight from the dish.

Preparation: 1 hour.

MENU 97

Ratatouille
Steak tartare
Mixed salad
Peaches in Sangria

Shopping list

1 lb/450 g tenderloin/fillet of beef, freshly ground/minced ●
2 oz/50 g capers ● 4 eggs ● 1 onion ● small bunch radishes ●
1 eggplant/aubergine ● 2 zucchini/courgettes ● 3 peppers ●
2 large ripe tomatoes ● mixed salad ingredients ● small bunch
parsley ● basil ● 1 bottle strong red wine (e.g. Chianti or
Bordeaux) ● 1 orange ● 1 lemon ● 4 ripe yellow peaches.

From the store cupboard ● garlic – olive oil –
wine vinegar – superfine/caster sugar – sparkling
mineral water – salt – pepper – marjoram or
oregano.

Work schedule ● Soak the orange and lemon
rind in the sugar for the Sangria. Start cooking
the Ratatouille. Wash and drain the salad and
prepare the Steak tartare.

Ratatouille

1 medium-sized onion, finely chopped
3/2 tbsp olive oil
1 eggplant/aubergine, diced
2 zucchini/courgettes, cubed
3 medium-sized peppers, diced
2 large ripe tomatoes, skinned, seeded and diced
salt
pepper
juice of 1 clove garlic
finely chopped parsley
½ tbsp fresh basil, finely chopped, or a pinch of dried
½ tbsp fresh marjoram or oregano or a pinch of dried

Sauté the onion in oil and then add the eggplant/aubergine, zucchini/courgettes, peppers and tomatoes. Season with salt and pepper, cover and simmer over a low heat for 30-40 minutes, preferably without stirring. When the vegetables are tender, add the garlic juice, parsley, basil and the marjoram or oregano. Stir and ladle into a heated serving dish. Ratatouille is best eaten warm or cold.

Preparation: 50 minutes.

Steak tartare

1 lb/450 g tenderloin/fillet of beef, freshly ground/minced

salt
pepper
4 egg yolks
1 tbsp chopped capers
1 tbsp finely chopped onion
1 tbsp chopped parsley
4 radishes

Season the finely ground/minced or scraped meat with salt and pepper and shape into 4 flat rounds. Make a hollow and place an egg yolk in the center of each. Garnish with the chopped capers, onion and parsley and a decoratively cut radish.

Preparation: 10 minutes.

Peaches in Sangria

peel of 1 orange (no pith)
peel of 1 lemon (no pith)
4/3 tbsp superfine/caster sugar
1 orange, divided into segments
4 large ripe peaches, skinned
1 bottle strong red wine (e.g. Chianti or Bordeaux)
½ large bottle sparkling mineral water, chilled
1 dozen ice cubes

Place the orange peel, lemon peel and the sugar in a tall glass jug. Stir well with a long-handled spoon, pressing the peel so that it releases its essential oils into the sugar. Add the orange

segments, cover the jug and leave in a cool place for as long as possible. Just before serving, add the skinned peaches, the wine, the well-chilled mineral water and ice cubes. Use a ladle to transfer a peach with plenty of Sangria into each person's dish. This dessert provides a refreshing end to a summer meal; slice the peaches if preferred before adding to the Sangria.

Preparation: 15 minutes.
Refrigeration: 1 hour.

MENU 98

Onion flan
Turkey breasts Piedmont style
Creamed potatoes
Pineapple Johannesburg

Shopping list

1½ lb/700 g boned raw turkey breasts, cut into 4 slices ● 11 oz/300 g frozen shortcrust pastry ● 1 jar preserved ginger (in syrup) ● 1 ripe pineapple ● 8 walnuts ● 2 oz/50 g sweet almonds ● 2 large onions ● 3 eggs ● 7 fl oz/200 ml heavy/double cream ● 18 fl oz/500 ml milk ● 1 can or packet instant creamed potatoes ● 1 small white truffle.

From the store cupboard ● butter – flour – nutmeg – Marsala – Parmesan cheese – sugar or clear honey – kirsch or maraschino – salt – pepper.

Work schedule ● Prepare the pineapple and chill in the refrigerator. Start preparing the Onion flan. Cook the turkey breasts and make the creamed potatoes.

Onion flan

2 large onions
scant ½ cup/3½ oz/100 g butter
1 tbsp flour
3 eggs
1 cup/7 fl oz/200 ml heavy/double cream
salt
freshly ground pepper
nutmeg
11 oz/300 g frozen shortcrust pastry

Chop the onions finely and sauté gently in butter

over a low heat until transparent. Turn off the heat and allow to cool. Stir in the flour, then the eggs and the cream. Mix well and season with salt, freshly ground pepper and a little grated nutmeg. Roll out the shortcrust pastry and use to line a buttered pie plate/quiche dish 1½ in/4 cm deep. Pinch the overlapping pastry together to form a decorative border. Prick the bottom of the pastry with the prongs of a fork, pour in the onion mixture and bake in a preheated oven at 350°F/180°C/mk 4 for 30-40 minutes.

Preparation: 20 minutes.
Total time: 1 hour.

Turkey breasts Piedmont style

1½ lb/700 g boned raw turkey breasts, cut into 4 slices
flour
salt
pepper
¼ cup/2 oz/50 g butter
6/4 tbsp Marsala
1 small white truffle
3/2 tbsp freshly grated Parmesan cheese
2 tbsp stock

Pound the turkey slices with a meat bat; coat lightly with flour and season with salt and pepper. Fry in butter over a high heat until

minutes until the Parmesan cheese has melted.

Preparation: 20 minutes.

Pineapple Johannesburg

1 ripe pineapple
3 pieces preserved ginger
1-2 tbsp of the preserving syrup
8 shelled walnuts
1 tbsp sweet almonds, blanched and coarsely chopped
¹/₄ cup/2 fl oz/60 ml kirsch or maraschino liqueur

Slice off the top of the pineapple neatly so that it can be used as a lid for the finished dessert. Scoop out the flesh with a melon baller or cut into small cubes. Cut away and discard the tough central core of the fruit. Place the pineapple in a bowl with all the other ingredients, mix well and return to the pineapple shell; chill in the refrigerator for as long as possible before serving. Replace the top of the pineapple to form a decorative lid.

Preparation: 15 minutes.

golden brown. Drain and keep warm between two hot plates. Add the Marsala to the butter in the pan and boil until slightly reduced. Place the turkey slices in a shallow ovenproof dish, slice the white truffle into slivers and place on top; sprinkle with grated Parmesan cheese. Add the stock to the Marsala in the pan, pour over the turkey and place in a very hot oven for a few

MENU 99

Neuchâtel fondue
Pork chops with mustard sauce
Buttered Brussels sprouts
Fruit salad with lemon cream sauce

Shopping list

4 pork loin chops, thinly sliced ● 14 oz/400 g Gruyère cheese ● 1 egg ● 2 loaves French bread ● 1 small carton whipping cream ● 1 small carton light/single cream ● 1 large can fruit salad ● 1 lemon ● 1 lb/450 g Brussels sprouts.

From the store cupboard ● flour – garlic – dry white wine – kirsch – nutmeg – clarified butter (see p. 11) – onion – Dijon mustard – sugar – salt – pepper.

Work schedule ● Set out all the ingredients for the Neuchâtel fondue. Steam the Brussels sprouts. Prepare the fruit salad. Cook the pork chops and toss the Brussels sprouts in butter.

Neuchâtel fondue

14 oz/400 g Gruyère cheese
1 tbsp flour
1 clove garlic
1 cup/9 fl oz/200 ml dry white wine
salt

pepper
nutmeg
3/2 tbsp kirsch
French bread, cut into large cubes

Shred/grate the Gruyère cheese and mix with the flour. Rub the inside of the fondue dish with the cut clove of garlic. Pour in the wine, bring almost to boiling point and add the Gruyère cheese; stir continuously with a balloon whisk until the cheese has completely melted. Season with salt, freshly ground pepper and a pinch of nutmeg. When the cheese mixture starts to boil, stir in the kirsch; take the fondue dish to the table and set on the lighted spirit lamp. Provide each guest with a fondue fork and a supply of bread. The melted cheese must be kept very hot.

Preparation: 10 minutes.

a high heat. Remove the chops, drain and keep warm between two hot plates. Sauté the onion gently in the butter and juices in the pan. Stir in the mustard and add the wine; boil until reduced by half. Pour in the cream and reduce slightly. Return the meat to the pan for a minute or two, turning once to coat with the sauce.

Preparation: 15 minutes.

Fruit salad with lemon cream sauce

6/4 tbsp whipping cream
1 egg, separated
2 tbsp lemon juice
1 tsp superfine/caster sugar
pinch salt
1 can fruit salad

Whip the cream but do not sweeten. Whisk the egg white and then fold gently into the whipped cream with a metal spoon. Beat the egg yolk until it is light and creamy, then stir in the lemon juice, sugar and a pinch of salt. Beat well until the sugar has completely dissolved; fold in the whipped cream and egg white mixture very gently. Turn the fruit salad into a large crystal bowl and cover with the sauce.

Preparation: 15 minutes.

Pork chops with mustard sauce

4 pork loin chops, thinly sliced
salt
pepper
1 tbsp flour
3/2 tbsp clarified butter
1 onion, finely chopped
1 tbsp Dijon mustard
2/3 cup/5 fl oz/150 ml dry white wine
1/2 cup/3 1/2 fl oz/100 ml light/single cream

Season the meat with salt and pepper, coat lightly with flour and fry in clarified butter over

MENU 100

Game pâté in puff pastry
Veal loin chops with sage and white wine
Buttered spinach
Angels on horseback

Shopping list

4 7-oz/200-g veal loin chops ● 5 oz/150 g frozen or fresh puff pastry ● 16 large oysters ● 1 small can game pâté (hare, duck, pheasant, etc.) ● 4 slices/rashers smoked streaky bacon ● 1 egg ● 1¾ lb/800 g potatoes ● fresh sage leaves ● 2¼ lb/1 kg fresh spinach or 1 packet frozen.

From the store cupboard ● butter – flour – dry white wine – fresh breadcrumbs – salt – pepper.

Work schedule ● Prepare the puff pastry starter and place in the oven. Shuck the oysters and prepare for cooking. Cook the chops and the spinach. Heat the puff pastry and sandwich a layer of pâté between the two layers. Place the Angels on horseback in the oven just before serving the main course.

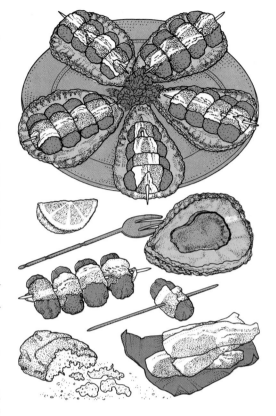

Game pâté in puff pastry

5 oz/150 g puff pastry
1 egg
1 small can game pâté (hare, duck, pheasant, etc.)

Roll out the puff pastry ⅛ in/2-3 mm thick and cut into rectangles 2 × 4 in/5 × 10 cm. Arrange the pastry rectangles on a dampened baking sheet and prick the pastry with a fork; brush with beaten egg and bake in a preheated oven at 350°F/180°C/mk 4 for 10-12 minutes. Prise the puff pastry rectangles carefully apart and sandwich a slice of pâté, cut to the same size as the pastry, in between.

Preparation: 20 minutes.

Veal loin chops with sage and white wine

1¾ lb/800 g potatoes, peeled and scooped into balls with the larger end of a melon baller
4 7-oz/200-g veal loin chops
flour
¼ cup/2 oz/50 g butter
5 fresh sage leaves
6/4 tbsp dry white wine
salt
pepper

Boil the potato balls in salted water for 10 minutes. While they are cooking, dry the loin chops thoroughly with paper towels; coat lightly with flour and brown on both sides in very hot butter. When the chops have browned, add the drained potatoes and the sage leaves and continue cooking over a fairly low heat until the sage has become crisp. Discard the sage leaves; pour in the white wine, add the salt and pepper and simmer for a few minutes more until the veal chops are tender.

Preparation: 20 minutes.

Angels on horseback

16 large oysters
4 slices smoked streaky bacon, cut very thin
fresh breadcrumbs
2½ tbsp/generous 1 oz/30 g melted butter

Shuck the oysters and remove the meat. Roll each one in a piece of streaky bacon and thread on to a skewer (allow 4 per skewer). Place in a roasting pan and sprinkle with soft white breadcrumbs. Pour the melted butter over the oysters and place in a very hot oven preheated to 450°F/270°C/mk 8 for a few minutes, until the bacon fat has become transparent.

Preparation: 10 minutes.

List of recipes

Andalusian gazpacho, 47
Angels on horseback, 154
Aphrodite salad, 63
Apple turnovers, 46
Apricot fritters with brandy sauce, 59
Artichokes Clamart, 38
Artichokes vinaigrette, 95
Asparagus Milan style, 50
Asparagus with mayonnaise, 100
Asparagus with remoulade sauce, 82
Avgolemono (Greek chicken and lemon soup),
    146
Avocado and grapefruit starter, 122
Avocado fool, 102
Avocado with mustard vinaigrette, 60
Avocados à la Ritz, 13
Avocados with caviar, 39

Baked Alaska, 120
Baked avocados, 117
Baked bananas, 132
Baked peaches, 41
Baked porgy/sea bream or bass, 50
Baked potatoes with caviar, 44
Banana dessert, 128
Banana mousse, 81
Bananas flamed in kirsch, 25
Bananas in butter, 118
Beef Stroganoff, 24
Bitoks (Russian veal patties) with asparagus
    tips, 51
Blue cheese dressing, 92
Bombay curried scampi, 28
Bombay hamburgers, 16
Boula-boula (Tahitian soup), 100
Brandy sauce, 59
Bread and butter pudding, 148
Breaded chicken breasts, 26
Breaded chicken drumsticks, 73
Broiled/grilled pigeons, 134
Buttered ribbon noodles, 87

Calf's liver Berlin style, 59
Cantonese fried chicken, 128
Carpaccio (savoury raw beef), 119
Cauliflower and rice mould, 61
Champagne chicken, 133
Champagne risotto, 13
Chawan Mushi (Japanese chicken, fish and egg
    soup), 22
Cheese choux puffs, 48
Cheese-filled pancakes, 105
Chestnut cream gâteau, 56
Chicken à la chasseur, 33
Chicken à la King, 85
Chicken breasts Caruso, 99
Chicken Calcutta, 78
Chicken legs with goose liver pâté, 142
Chicken Maryland salad, 136
Chicken paprika Hungarian style, 93
Chicken Picasso, 63
Chilled avocado soup, 67
Chilli con carne, 24
Chinese crispy fried noodles (Chow Mein), 101
Chinese fondue, 48

Chinese fried rice, 123
Chinese sweet and sour pork (T'ang Ts'u P'ai
    Ku), 124
Chippenham cheese savoury, 112
Clam chowder, 124
Coating batter, 33
Consommé à la reine, 51
Consommé Célestine, 109
Copacabana banana fritters, 33
Corn on the cob, 28
Country soup, 69
Country style risotto, 84
Coupe Alexandra, 45
Crabe à la russe, 24
Cream of artichoke and pea soup, 76
Cream of pea soup, 33
Cream of spinach soup, 20
Creamed spinach, 16
Creole Jambalaya, 118
Crêpes Marquise, 45
Crêpes Suchard, 30
Crêpes Suzette, 77
Crispy chicken breasts, 66
Curried Arabian veal, 110

Dubliner (ice cream, coffee and whiskey
    dessert), 73
Duchesse potatoes, 82
Duchesse tomatoes, 135

Entrecôte steaks with piquant sauce, 65
Entrecôte steaks with pizzaiola sauce, 42
Escalopes de veau Cordon Bleu, 14

Fillets of John Dory with capers, 96
Fillets of sole Saint-Germain, 100
Fleuret à la Riche, 121
Fondue Bourguignonne, 22
Fried chicken with lemon and herbs, 68
Fruit and cheese salad, 127
Fruit salad with Grand Marnier, 92
Fruit salad with lemon cream sauce, 153

Game pâté in puff pastry, 154
George's rigatoni, 43
George's scampi kebabs, 57
George's spaghetti, 137
Gin and grapefruit cocktail, 25
Glazed onions, 133
Gnocchi Paris style, 114
Goose liver pâté in puff pastry, 133
Gorgonzola cheese with honey, 95
Grapefruit and vodka cocktail, 43
Grilled filet mignon, 113
Guinea fowl with Champagne, 102

Hake Colbert, 112
Ham and sausages with sauerkraut, 106
Ham salad, 49
Hamburgers with pizzaiola sauce, 31
Hawaiian chicken salad, 79
Hawaiian gâteau, 94
Hawaiian ham, 20
Horseradish sauce, 23
Hot Vichyssoise, 27

Hovdessert (ice cream with meringues and hot chocolate sauce), 129

Ice cream sundae with chocolate sauce, 142
Indian dressing, 28
Individual rum babas with ice cream, 123
Irinka (Russian sweet chestnut and rum dessert), 122
Irish coffee, 27

Lamb chops/cutlets with cream and brandy, 80
Lamb chops with lemon and rosemary, 19
Liver and bacon with bacon-flavoured sautéed potatoes, 136
Liver with bacon and olives, 83
Lobster salad Tahiti, 145
Louis dressing, 41
Lychees with maraschino, 87

Macaroni with four cheeses, 32
Maître d'hôtel butter, 112
Mangoes flamed in liqueur, 83
Maryland crab salad, 59
Meat kebabs with oriental pilaf rice, 56
Melon and port cocktail, 73
Melon and shrimp/prawns Polynesian style, 40
Melon with port, 25
Meringues Negrita, 104
Mimosa salad, 30
Minestrone soup, 74
Minted peas, 81
Mushroom salad, 15
Mussel kebabs, 109
Mussels Dieppe style, 140

Neuchâtel fondue, 152

Omelette soufflée with peas, 57
Onion flan, 151
Oriental pilaf rice, 56
Oysters poached in Champagne, 130

Palm hearts with Parmesan and hot butter dressing, 76
Palm hearts with vinaigrette dressing, 34
Pancakes Cevennes style, 51
Pancakes with Emmental cheese, 52
Paprika pork chops with sauerkraut, 69
Parmentier soup, 39
Peach Melba, 23
Peaches Alexandra, 106
Peaches flamed in rum, 20
Peaches in Sangria, 150
Peaches Sobieski, 59
Pears flamed in brandy, 134
Pears flamed in rum, 68
Pears with chocolate sauce, 145
Peking lobster, 99
Peppered entrecôte steaks, 94
Peppers in sweet and sour sauce, 137
Peppers with anchovies and garlic, 14
Philippine chicken salad, 38
Pigeons en cocotte, 97
Pilaf rice, 29
Pineapple Johannesburg, 152

Pizzaiola sauce, 31
Poached salmon steaks, 148
Poires belle Hélène, 79
Pommes de terre noisette, 21
Porgy/gilt head bream en papillote, 91
Pork chops Bavarian style, 75
Pork chops with mustard sauce, 153
Pork steaks with mustard, 92
Potato and tomato soup, 66
Potato croquettes, 147
Prague croquettes, 28
Prosciutto/raw ham with melon or figs, 19

Quail and sausage kebabs, 87
Quails with cream, 141
Quails with olives, 109
Quiche Lorraine, 83
Quick-fried steaks, 46
Quick hamburgers, 147
Quick pancakes, 30
Quick veal in cream and wine sauce, 86

Rainbow sundae, 136
Raspberries Melba, 55
Raspberry mousse, 115
Ratatouille, 150
Ribbon noodles with butter and sage, 104
Ribbon noodles with ham and mushrooms, 96
Ribbon noodles with prosciutto/raw ham, 70
Rich sponge gâteau, 37
Risotto alla Milanese, 37
Risotto with Barolo wine, 128
Risotto with Gorgonzola cheese, 65
Risotto with scampi and brandy, 116
Roast chicken with rosemary, 21
Roast chicken with tarragon, 139
Rognons Robert, 63
Roman chicken and egg soup, 42
Rossolnick (Russian cucumber soup), 139

Salade niçoise, 113
Saltimbocca alla salvia (veal, ham and sage rolls), 64
Savoury pancakes, 97
Savoury tuna toasts, 78
Seafood curry, 19
Scampi cocktail, 26
Scampi flamed in whisky, 79
Shrimp/prawns Tourkolimano (Greek style), 127
Shrimp/prawns with mayonnaise, 62
Singapore kebabs, 122
Singapore sundae, 86
Smoked eel with fried egg, 55
Smoked herring starter, 21
Smoked trout with horseradish sauce, 23
Snails bourguignonne (Burgundy style), 58
Sole fillets Florentine, 25
Sole meunière, 62
Soupe à l'oignon, 15
Spaghetti alla carbonara, 14
Spaghetti with bacon and Parmesan cheese, 73
Spaghetti with cheese and pepper, 64
Spaghetti with compressed smoked roe, 49
Spaghetti with garlic, oil and chilli pepper, 29

Spatchcock chickens, 145
Spiced calf's liver, 37
Spring chicken with white wine, 117
Steak au poivre, 30
Steak Diane, 13
Steak in beer, 132
Steak tartare, 150
Steamed buttered leeks, 88
Steamed potatoes, 40
Strawberries and cream, 99
Strawberries Romanoff, 50
Strawberries with Grand Marnier, 138
Strawberry mousse, 135
Stuffed chicken breasts, 129
Stuffed eggs, 79
Stuffed fillet of beef Russian style, 118
Sukiyaki, 130
Sweet and sour onions, 114
Swiss salad, 42

Taramasalata, 121
Thousand island dressing, 55
Tomato vinaigrette, 95
Tortellini with cheese sauce, 120
Tournedos flamed in brandy, 32
Tournedos Marquis de Sade, 44
Tropicana melon cocktail, 88
Trout baked in red wine, 76
Trout Caprice, 121
Trout with almonds, 40
Turkey breasts Hungarian style, 137
Turkey breasts Parisian style, 44
Turkey breasts Piedmont style, 151
Turkey breasts with cheese and ham, 84
Turkey slices in Marsala sauce, 47

Veal and bacon kebabs, 115
Veal chops/cutlets Milanese, 52
Veal chops Provençale, 41
Veal cutlets/escalopes with Calvados, 138
Veal cutlets/escalopes with lemon sauce, 38
Veal cutlets/escalopes with Madeira sauce, 58
Veal loin chops with sage and white wine, 154
Veal medallions with orange sauce, 82
Veal rissoles with pizzaiola sauce, 70
Veal steaks with Armagnac, 101
Venison steaks with cream and brandy sauce,
    104
Viennese sundae, 98
Vinaigrette dressing, 34

White Lady sundae, 103
Wiener Schnitzel, 61

Zucchini/courgettes with garlic and parsley, 64

Recommended Wines

Menu	*Menu*

<table>
<tr><td>

1 Italian Riesling, Chablis, Chianti, Burgundy
2 Pinot grigio, Pouilly-Fuissé, Rubino
3 Dry Italian or French Rosé
4 Gavi, Torgiano, Cabernet
5 Verdicchio, Muscadet
6 Sauvignon, Sancerre, Grignolino, Vouvray
7 Cortese di Gavi, Chablis, Grumello
8 Vernaccia di San Gimignano, Valpolicella, Merlot
9 Pomino, Bâtard Montrachet, Barbera, Ghemme
10 Tocai, Sylvaner
11 Pinot grigio, Chablis
12 Frascati Classico, Montefiascone, Château de Selle
13 Tocai Sauvignon
14 Barbera, Moulin à Vent
15 Lambrusco, Pommard
16 Pinot grigio, Ermitage (blanc), Grumello, Romanée Saint Vivant
17 Greco di Tufo, Castel del Monte Rosso
18 Mersault, Sassella, Châteauneuf du Pape
19 Vernaccia, Montrachet
20 Pomino, Prosecco
21 Verdicchio, Soave, Brunello, Gevrey Chambertin
22 Chablis, Gattinara, Grand Echézeaux
23 Prosecco, Cabernet, Fleurie
24 Barolo or Brunello di Montalcino
25 Orvieto, Beaujolais
26 Valpolicella, Bonnes Mares
27 Rhine Riesling, Tocai del Collio
28 Orvieto, Corton Charlemagne, Sangiovese, Beaujolais
29 Sauvignon, Rüdesheimer Rosengarten
30 Corvo Bianco, Chassagne Montrachet
31 Merlot, Cabernet, Sauvignon
32 Clastidio rosato
33 Cabernet Sauvignon, Riesling
34 Merlot, Clos Vougeot
35 Cinqueterre, Château Latour Blanche, Dolcetto
36 Verdicchio, Bâtard Montrachet
37 Orvieto, Mersault, Torgiano
38 Chablis, Malvasia, Nobile di Montepulciano
39 Bianco d'Alcamo, Rosso del Piglio
40 Nebbiolo, Fleurie
41 Pinot noir, Grand Echézeaux
42 Barbaresco, Chambolle Musigny
43 Cortese di gavi, Inferno, Bonnes Mares
44 Lambrusco
45 Villa Antinori bianco, Montrachet, Grignolino
46 Gavi, Torgiano, Rosé d'Anjou
47 Inferno, Grand Echézeaux
48 Chambolle Musigny Riesling

</td><td>

49 Cabernet Trentino, Romanée Saint Vivant
50 Orvieto, Torgiano, Traminer
51 Cortese di Gavi, a young Merlot
52 Corton Charlemagne, Gewürztraminer
53 Bâtard Montrachet, Taurasi
54 Monsupello d'Oltrepò Pavese
55 Prosecco di Conegliano
56 Spumante nature
57 Soave Classico, Barolo
58 Château de Selle, rosé
59 Hospice de Beaune, Barbaresco
60 Sangue di Giuda, Sangiovese
61 Gattinara, Grand Echézeaux
62 Cortese, Chambolle Musigny
63 A young Nebbiolo
64 Rhine Riesling, Chassagne Montrachet
65 Sparkling dry white wine
66 Champagne (Brut) or dry Italian Spumante
67 Riesling, Cabernet
68 Sauvignon, Graves, Grumello, Chambertin
69 Lambrusco
70 A young Locorontondo
71 Tocai, Château Latour Blanche
72 Pinot grigio, Ermitage blanc
73 Vernaccia, Château Haut Brion, Barbera, Moulin à Vent
74 Riesling, Bâtard Montrachet
75 Cortese, Graves, Bernkasteler, Bardolino
76 Rosso Sangiovese
77 Sauvignon, Graves, Sassella, Clos Vougeot
78 Pomino, Mersault, Frascati
79 Graves supérieures blanc, Barbaresco
80 Sylvaner
81 Cortese, Rüdesheimer, Grignolino, Aloxe Corton
82 Bâtard Montrachet
83 Barolo, Chambertin
84 Champagne or Italian Spumante Classico
85 Pinot grigio, Ermitage blanc, Gattinara, Grand Echézeaux
86 Champagne or Italian Spumante Classico
87 Pinot bianco, Chablis, Clos Vougeot
88 Sauvignon, Chassagne Montrachet
89 Italian Riesling, Ermitage (red or white), Dolcetto
90 Cortese, Vernaccia di Oristano (Sardinia)
91 Merlot, Volnay
92 Sauvignon, Graves, Sassella, Pommard
93 Spumante nature, Dolcetto
94 Tocai, Zeltinger, Clos Vougeot
95 Pouilly-Fuissé, Grumello, Gevrey Chambertin
96 Soave, Graves
97 Sangria Spanish wine cup (prepared according to recipe)
98 Château de Selle
99 Puligny Montrachet, Clos Vougeot
100 Pinot grigio, Pinot nero

</td></tr>
</table>